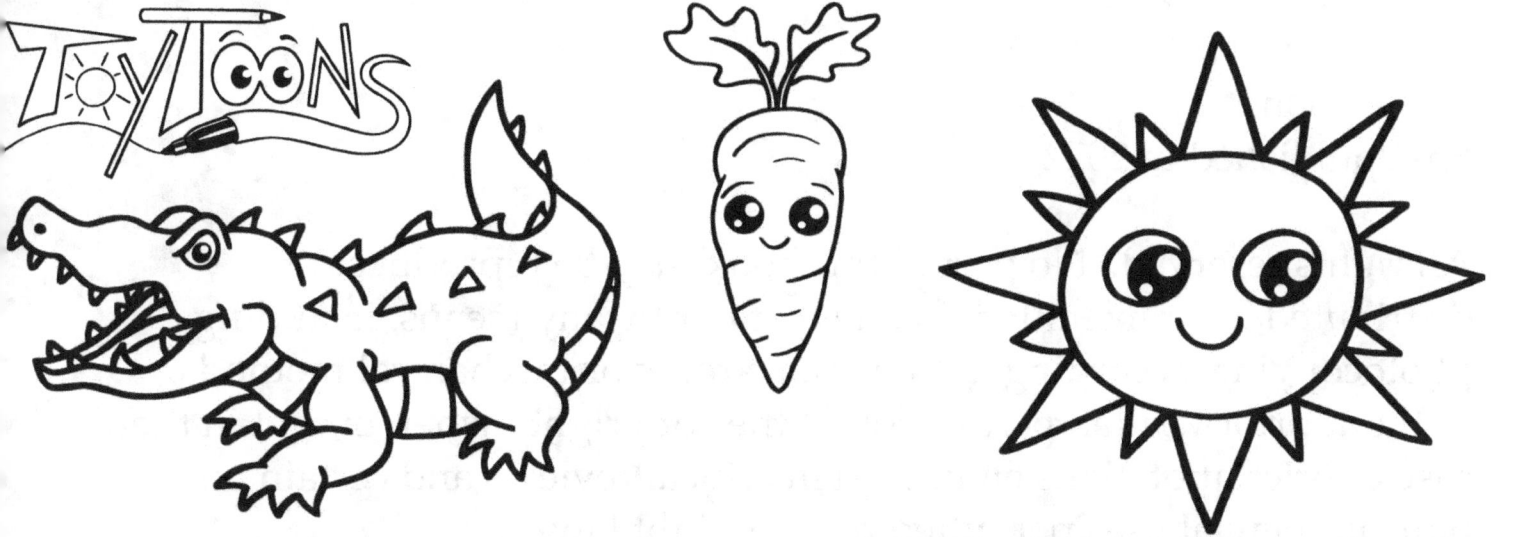

This book belongs to:

....

....

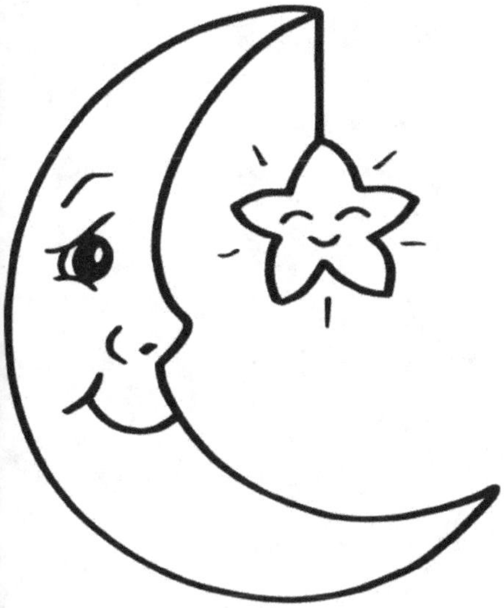

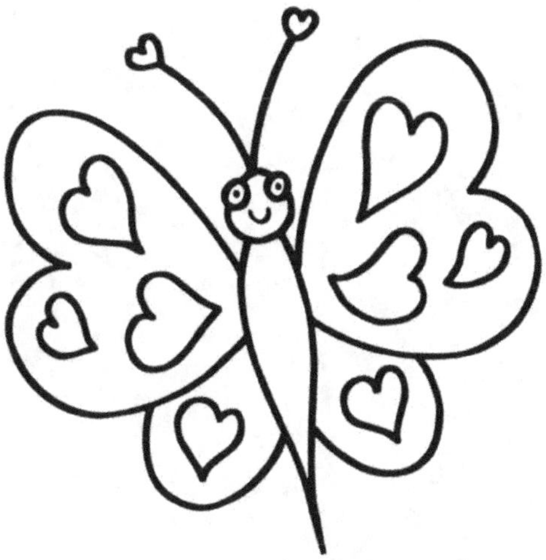

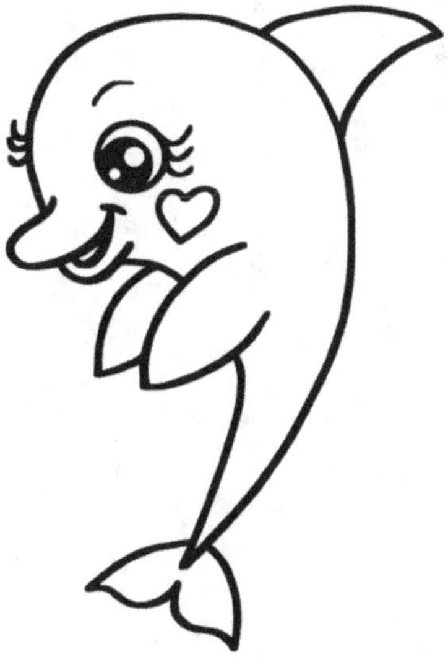

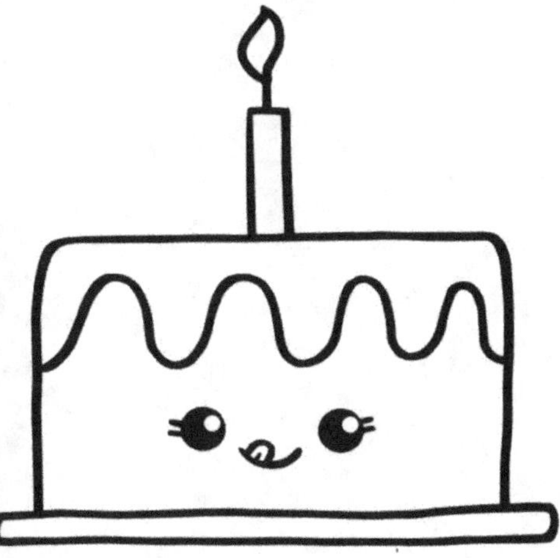

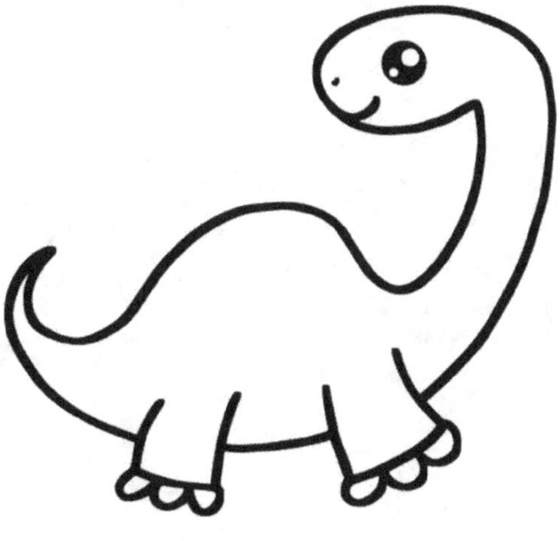

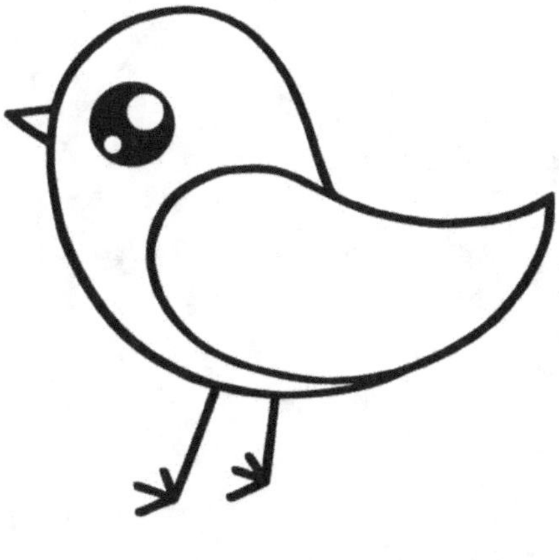

© ToyToons
First published in 2022

All rights reserved. No part of this book may be reproduced, distributed, or transmitted, in any form or by any means, including photocopying, recording, or other electronic or mechanical methods, without prior written permission of the copyright owner, except in the case of brief quotations embodied in critical reviews and certain other noncommercial uses permitted by copyright law.
For more information visit www.DrawingGuides.com

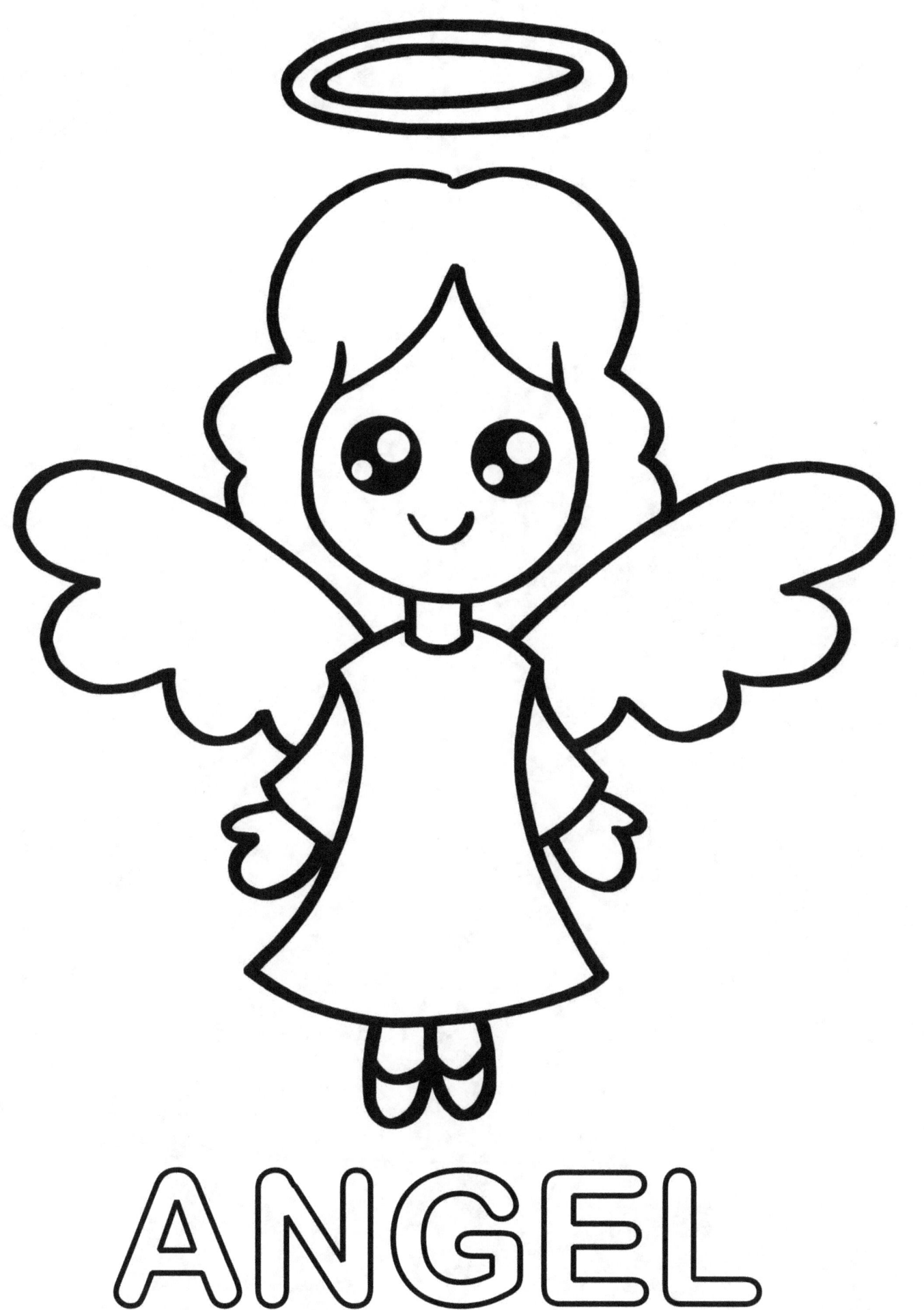

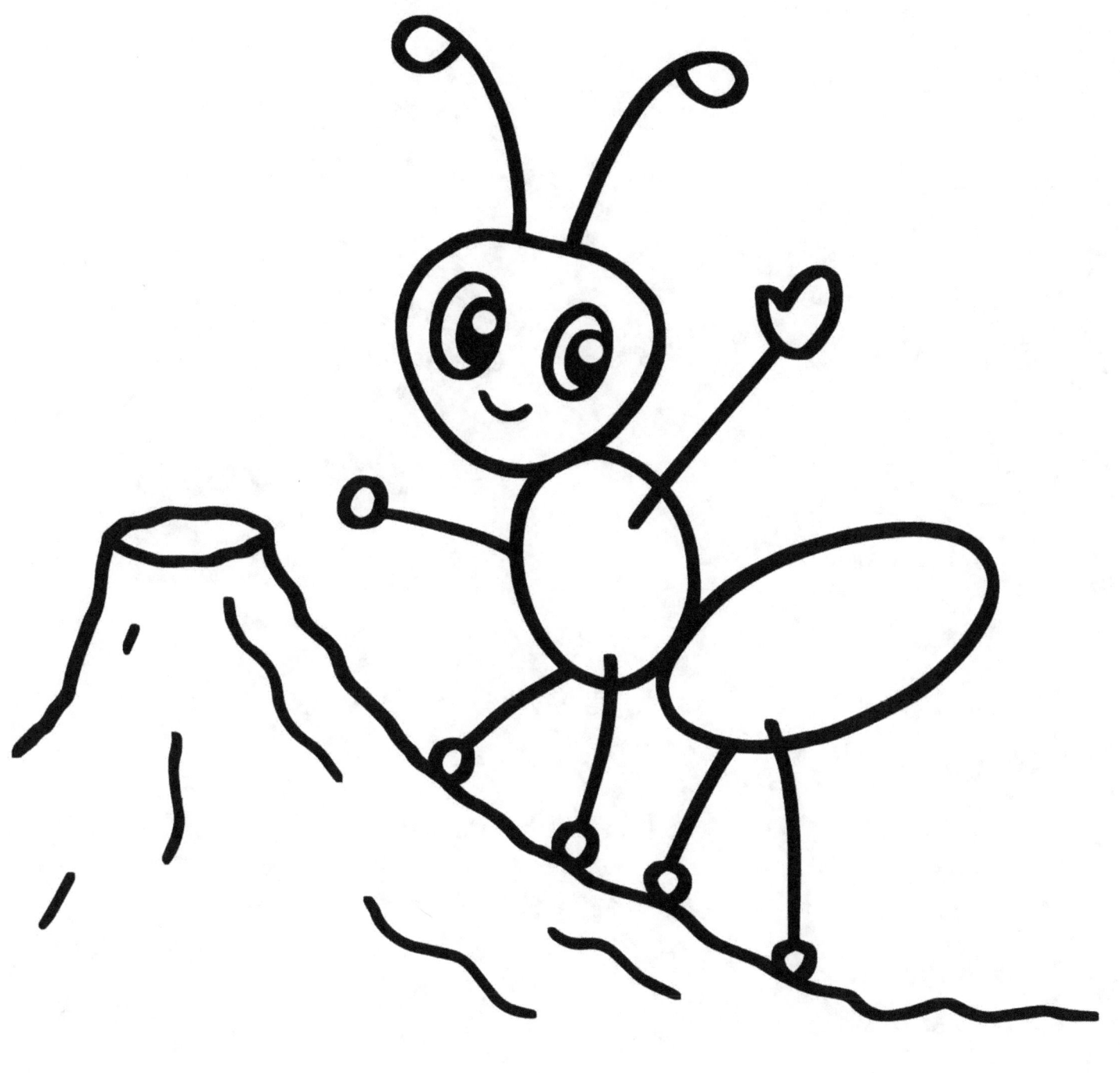

ANT

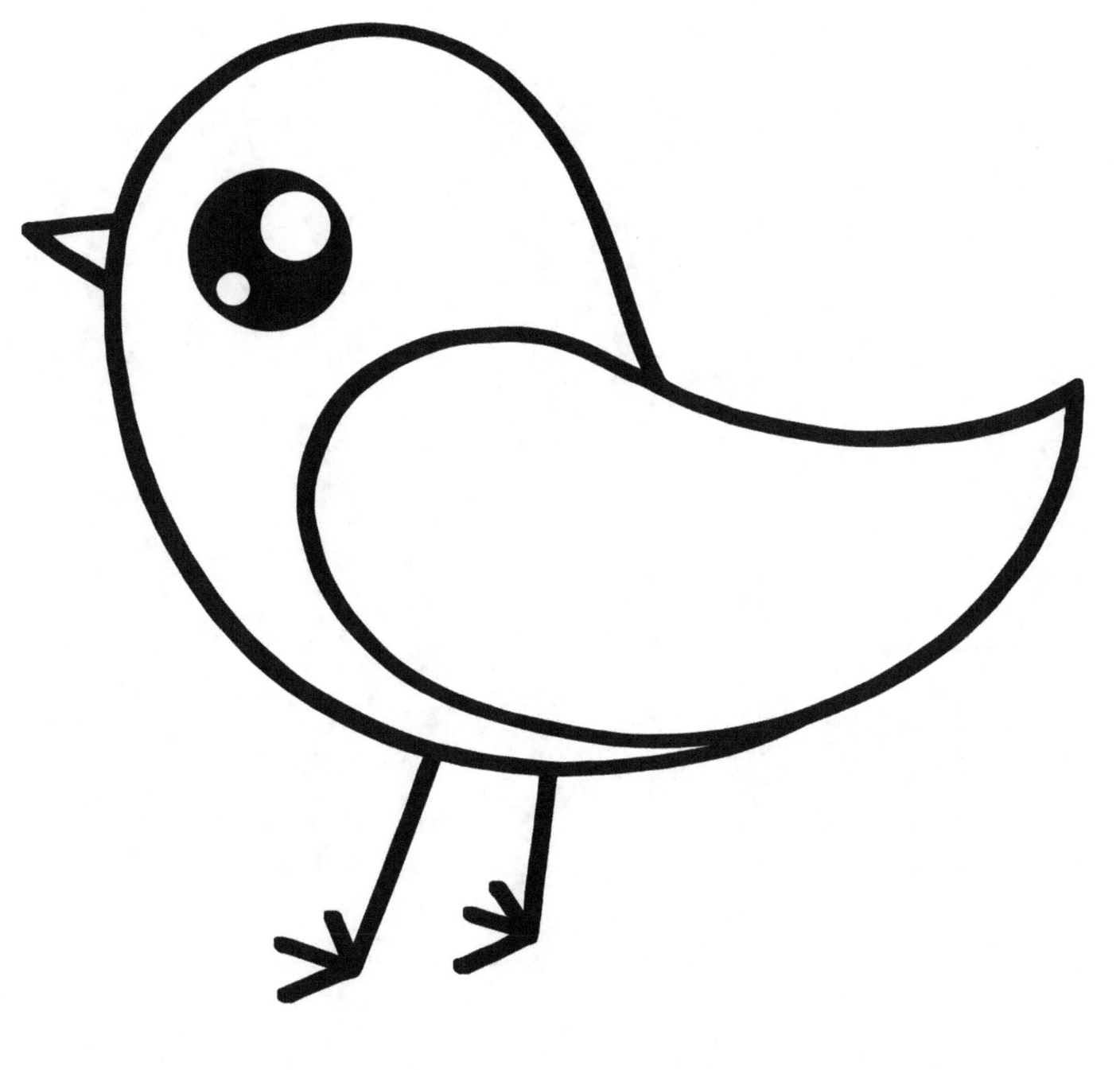

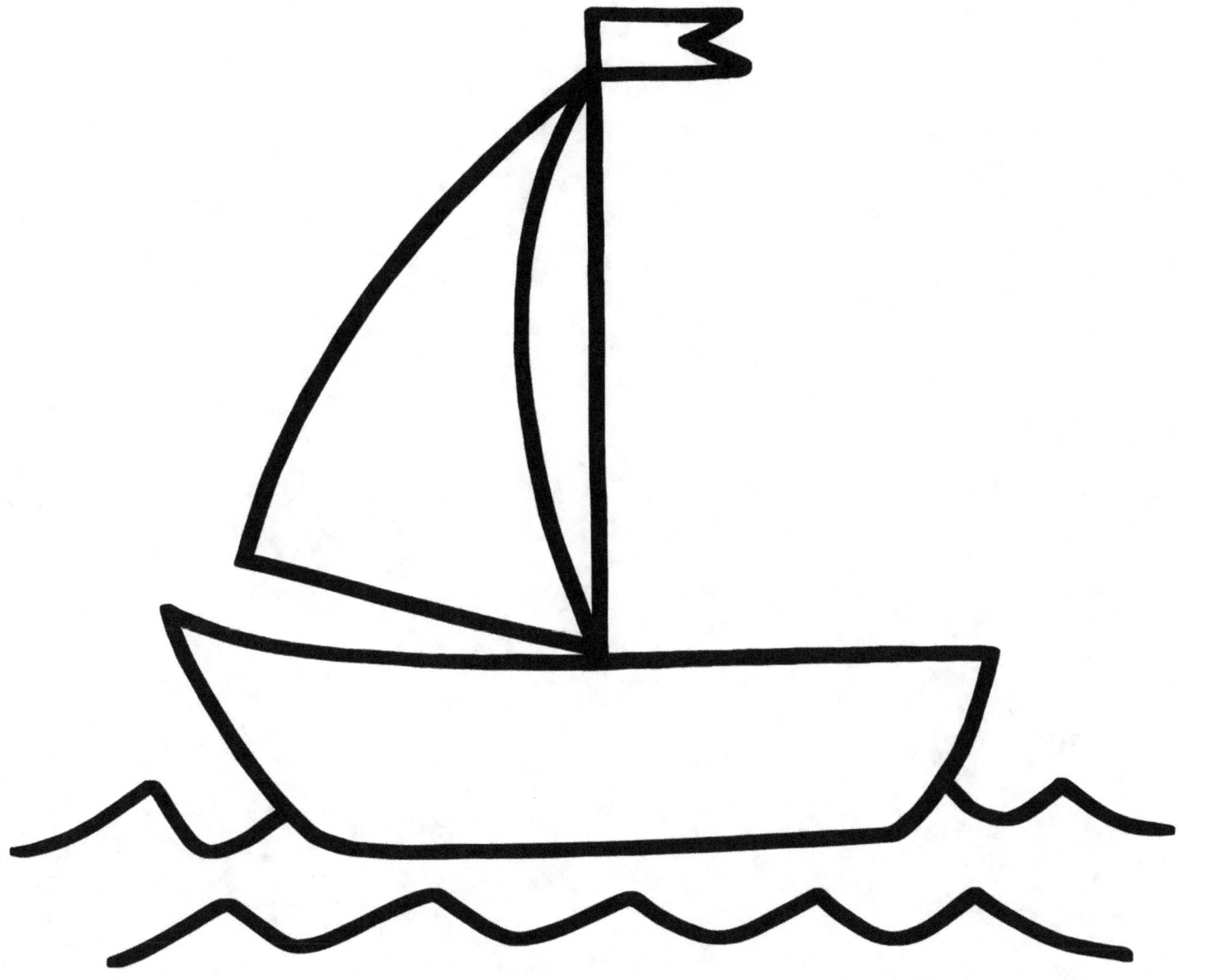

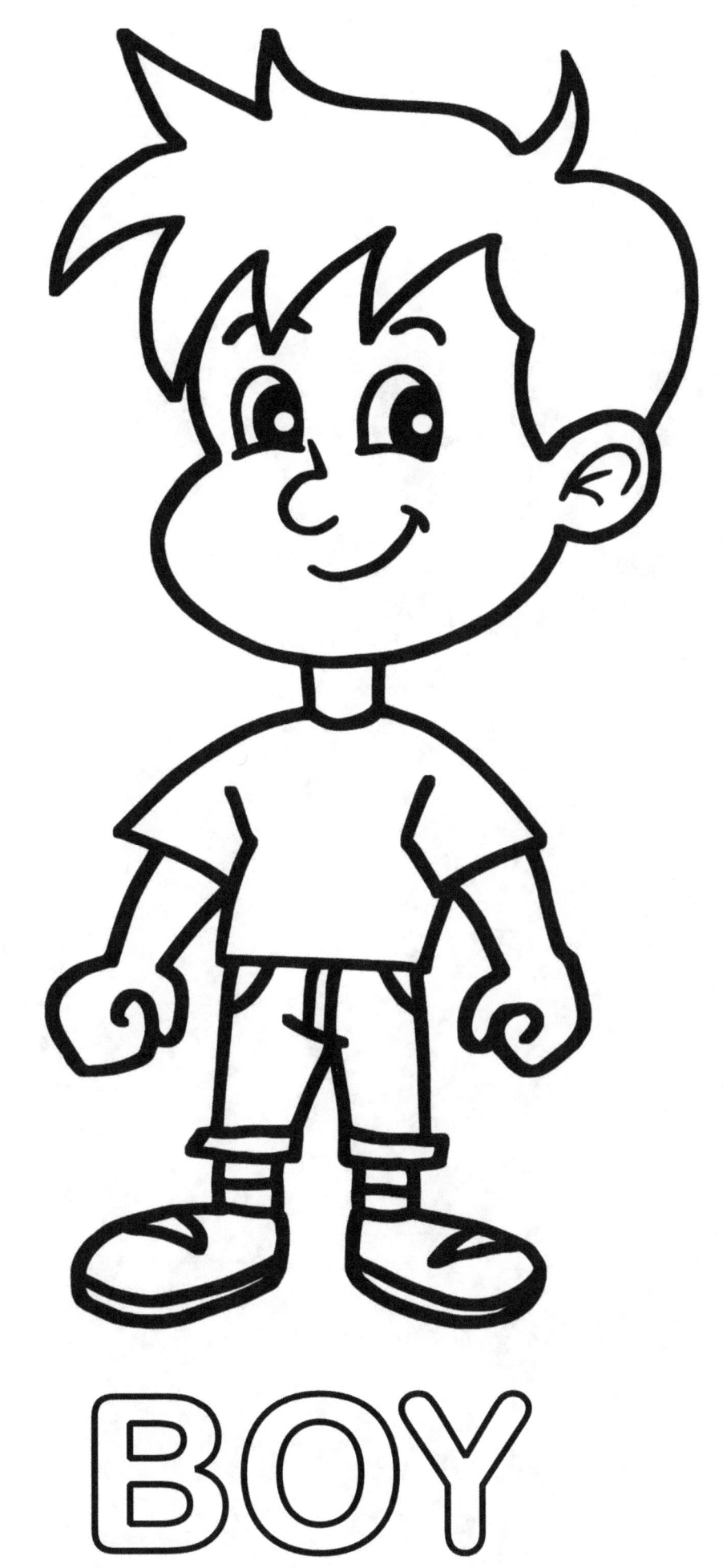

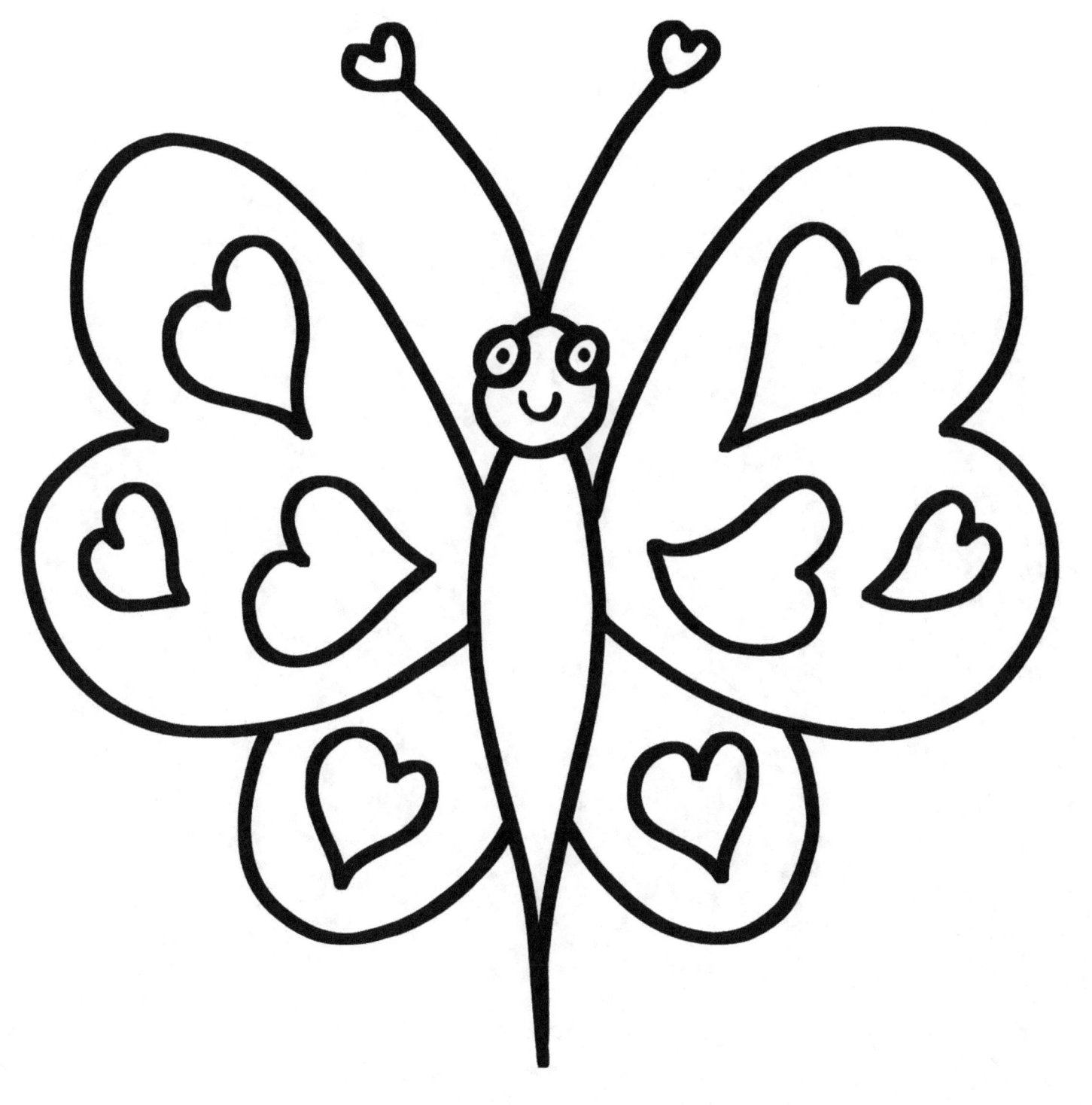

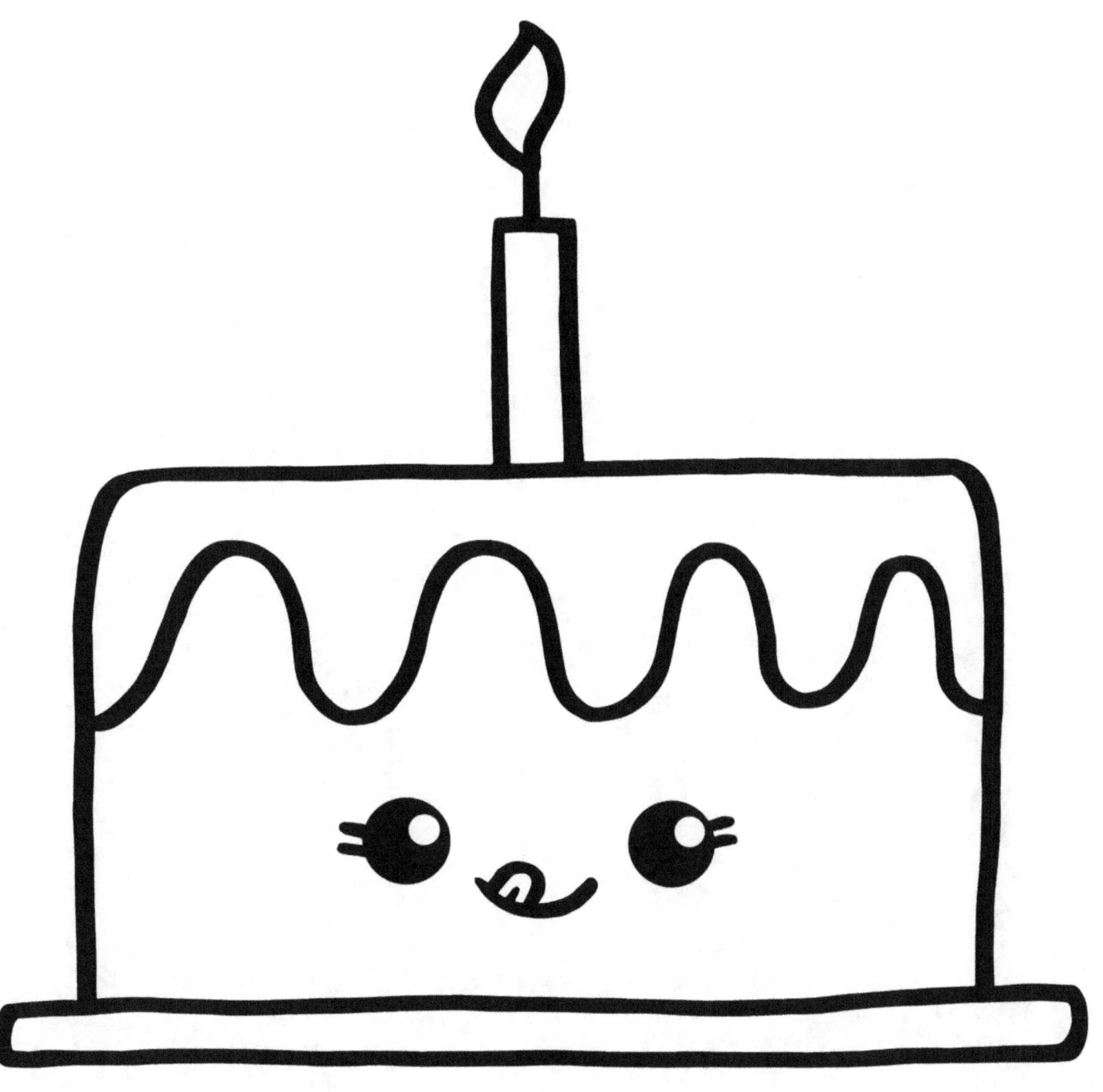

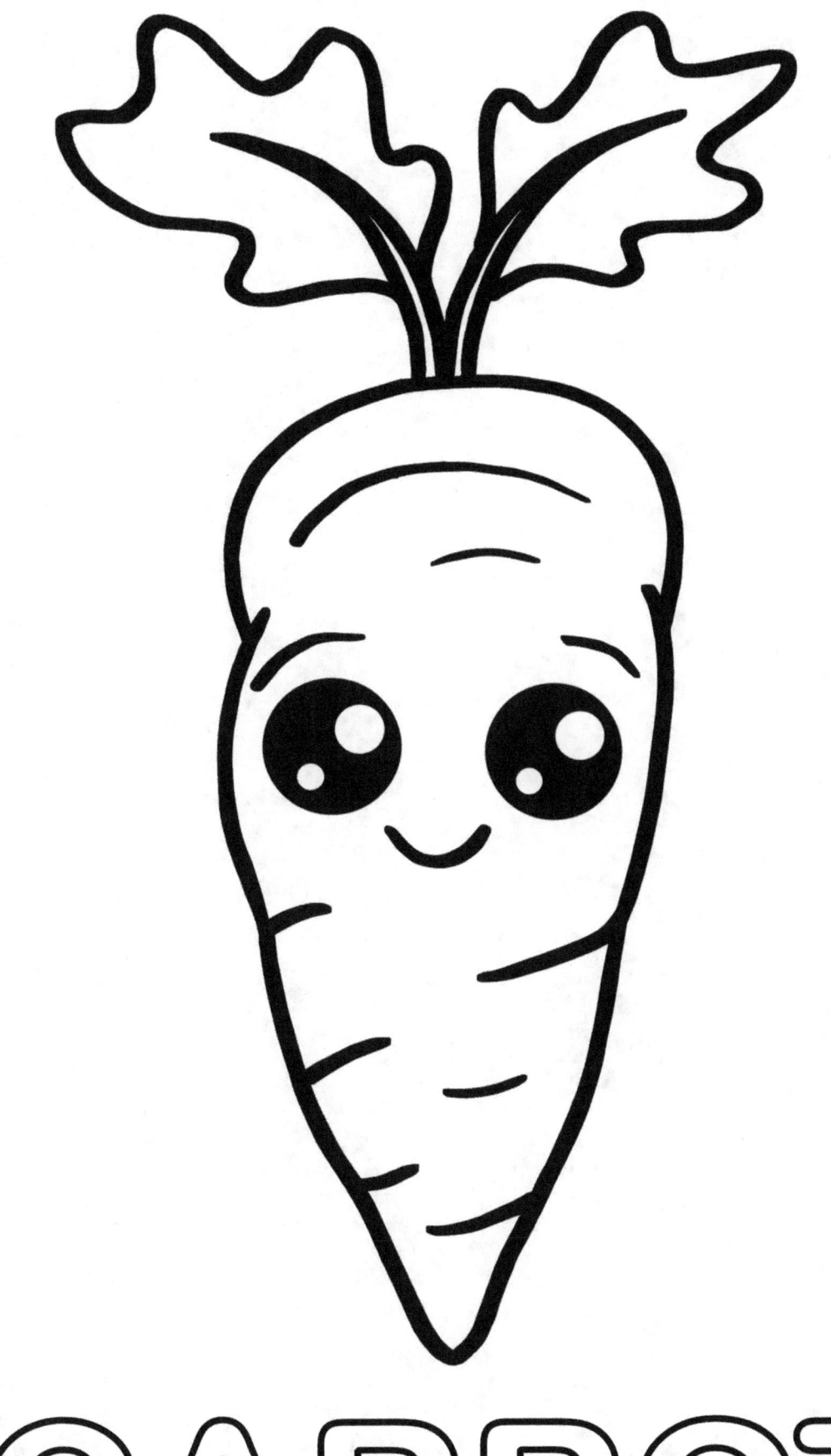

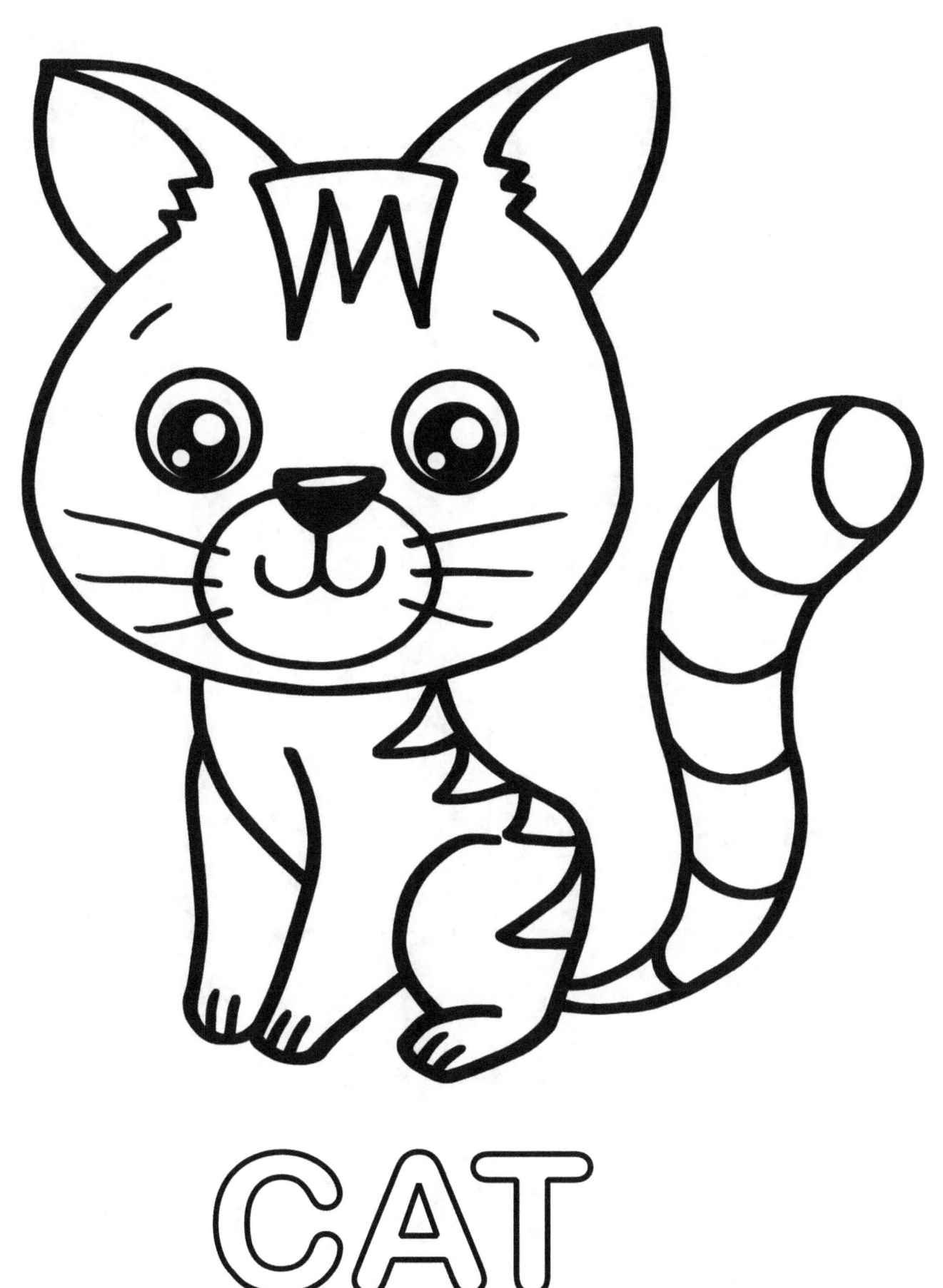

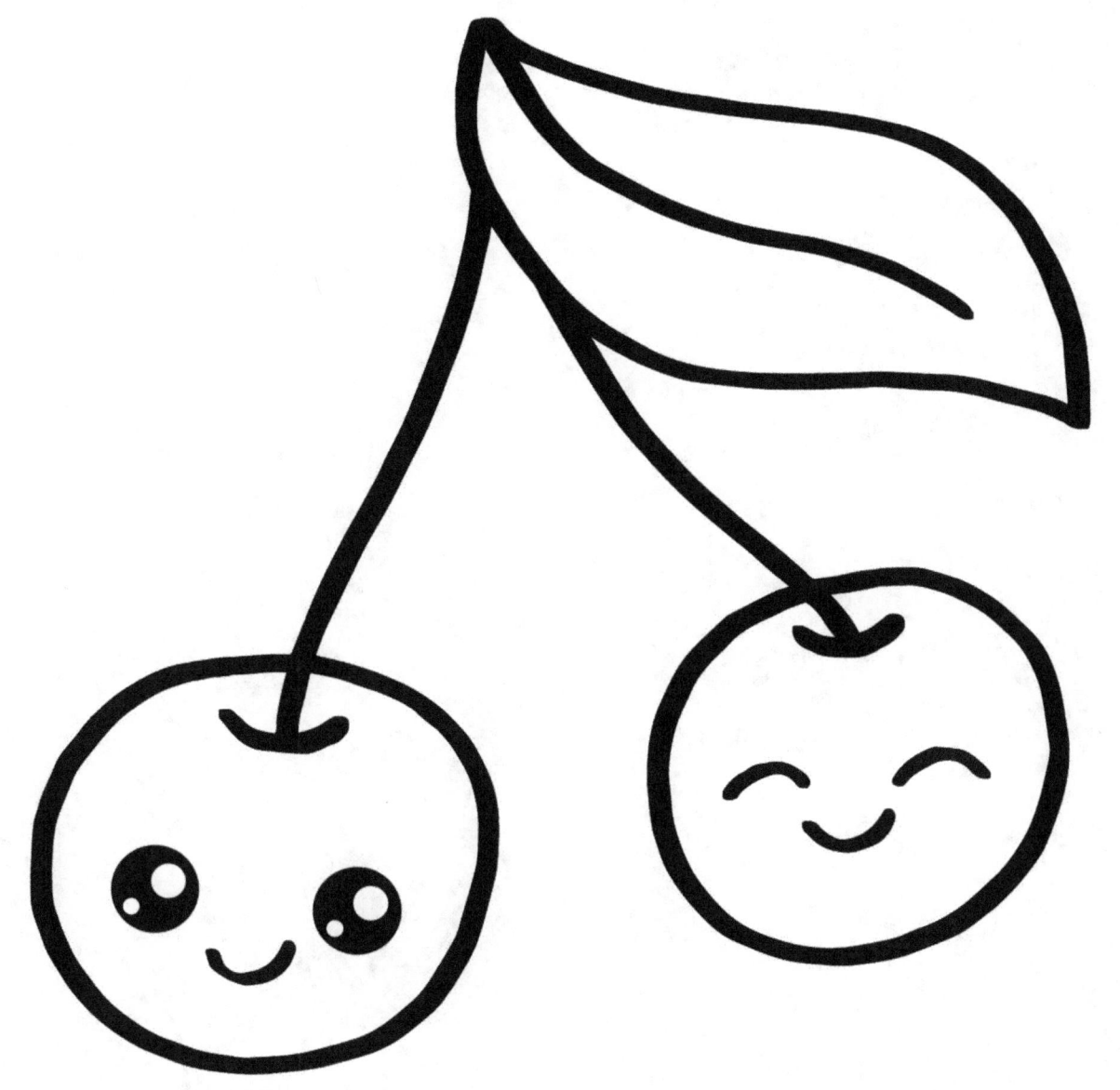

CHERRIES

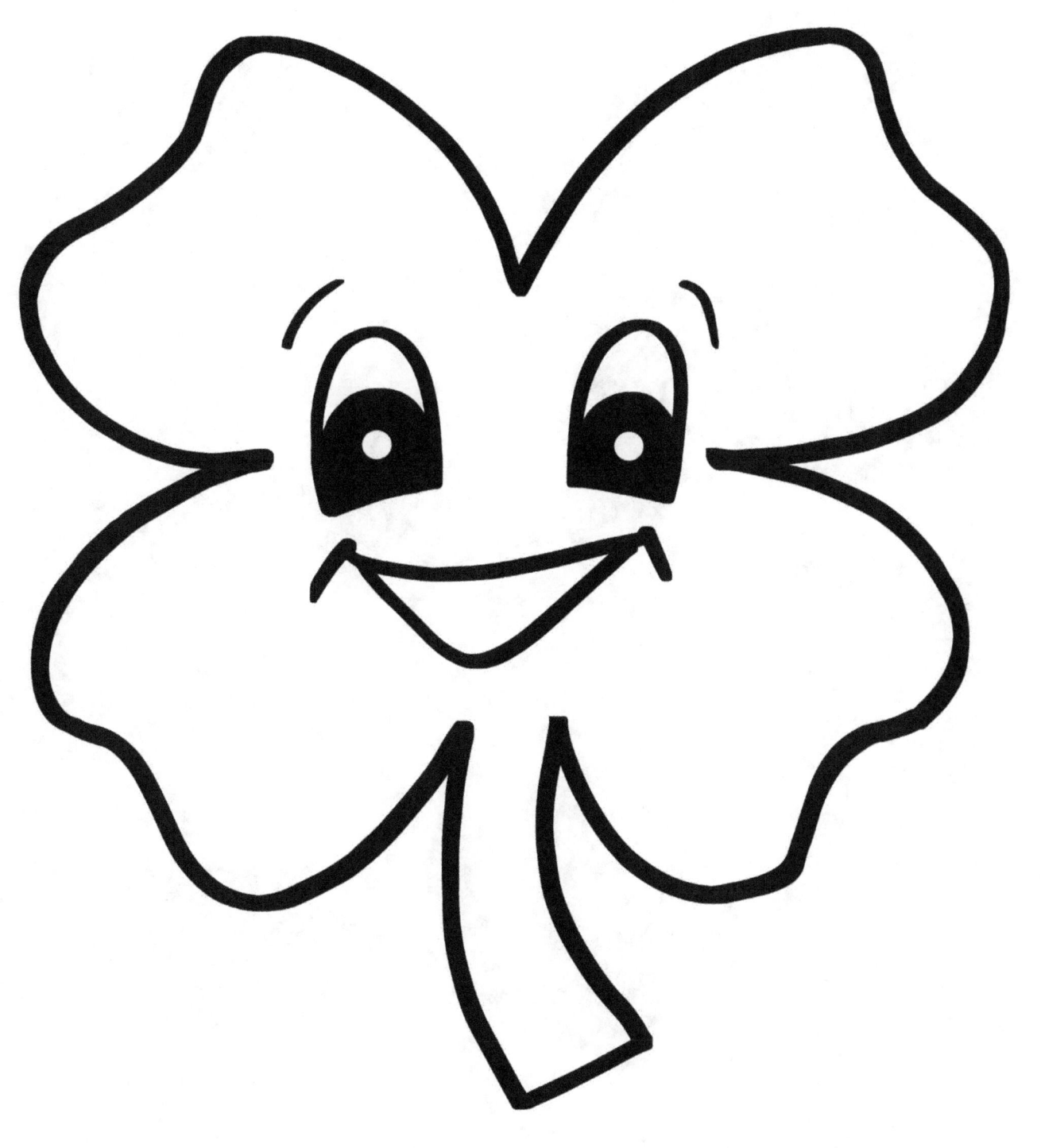

CLOVER

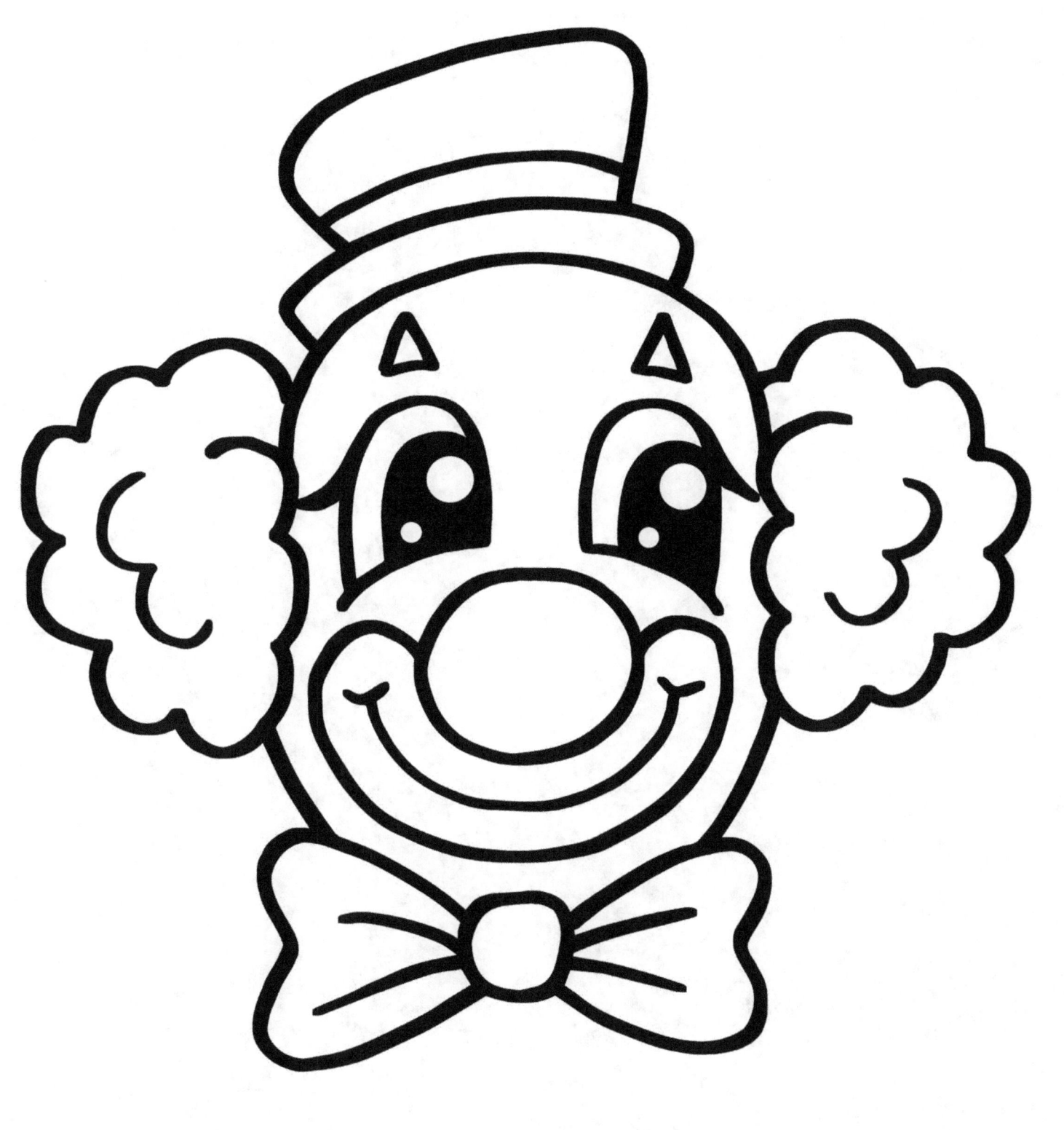

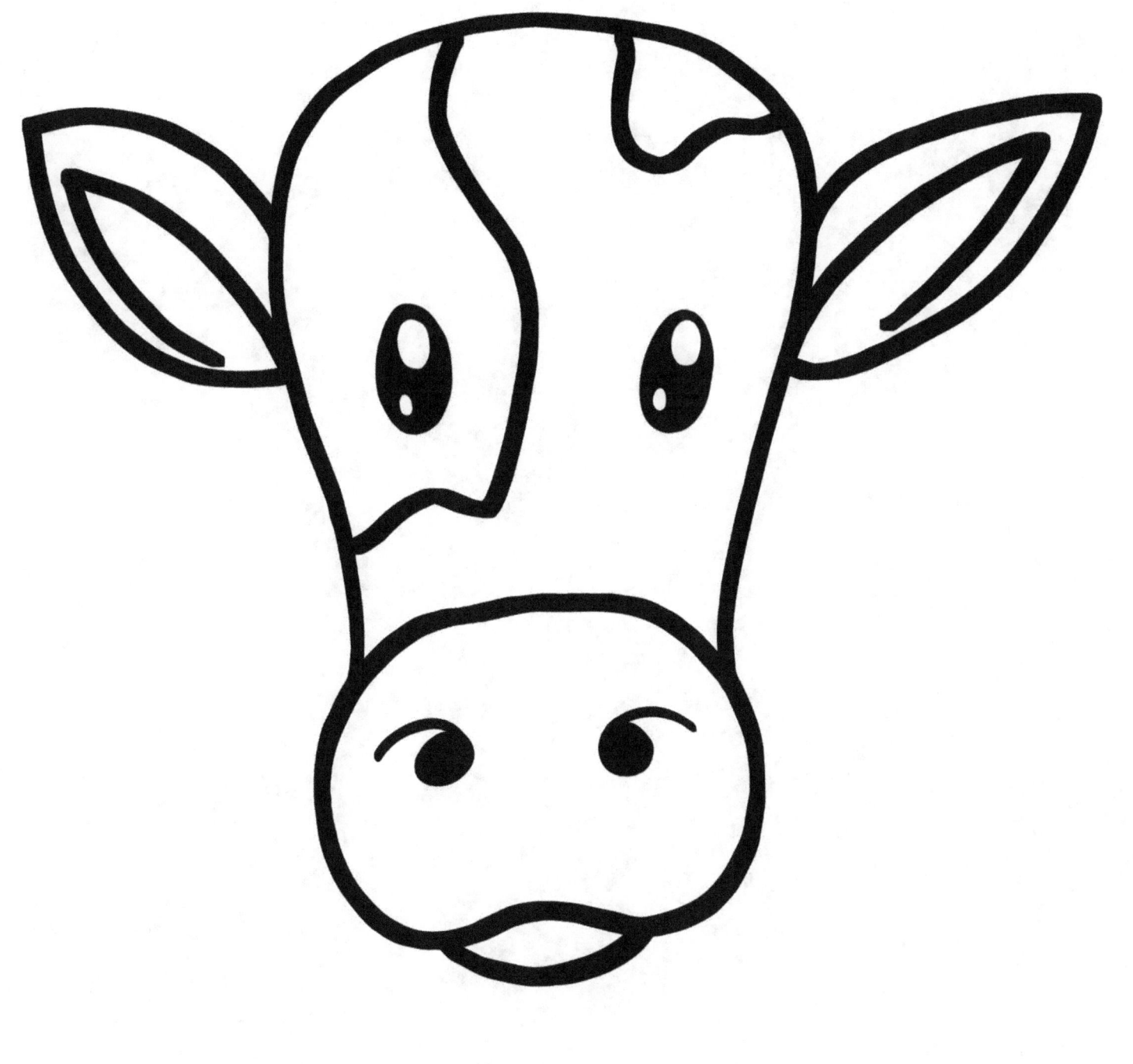

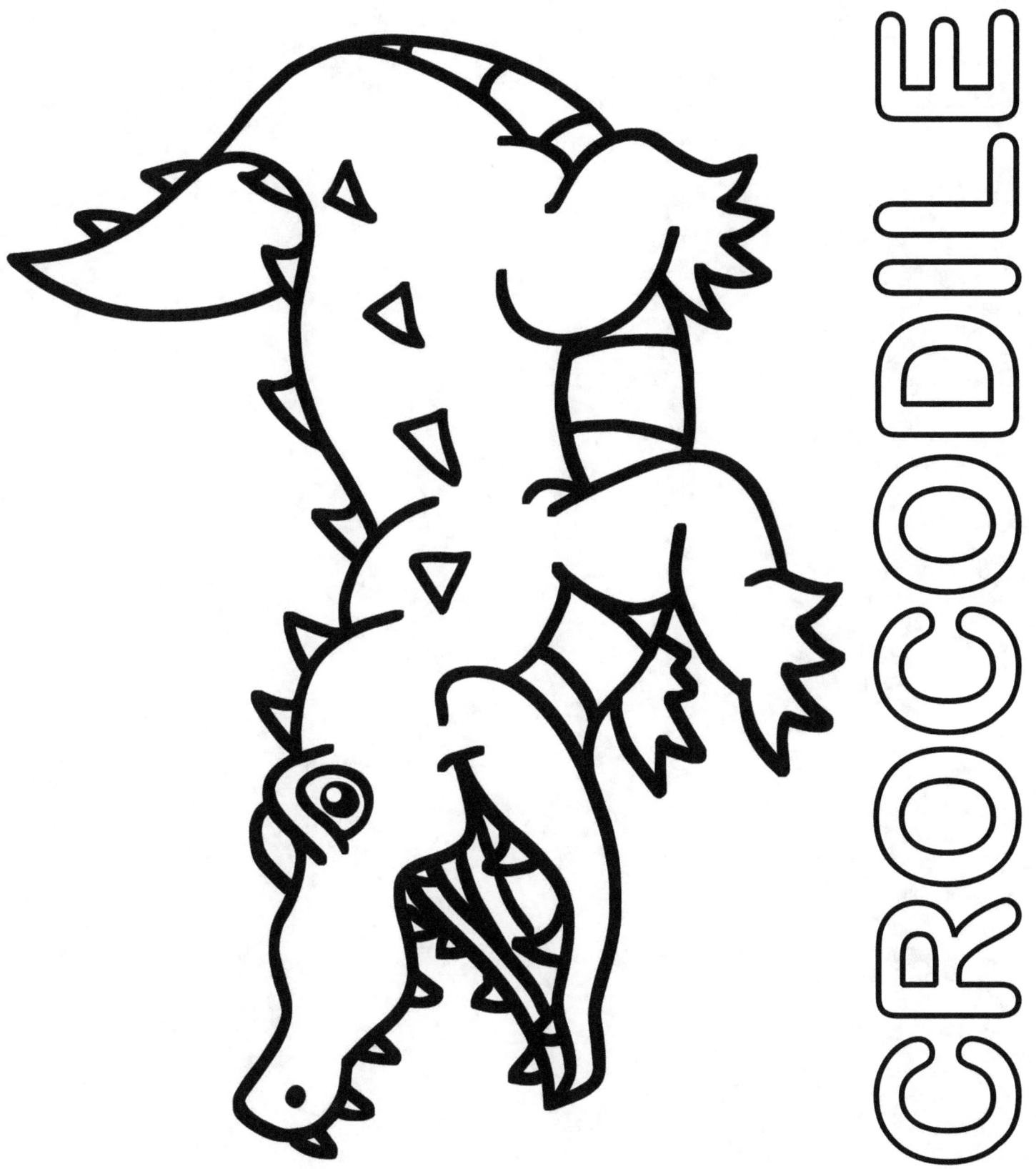

CROCODILE

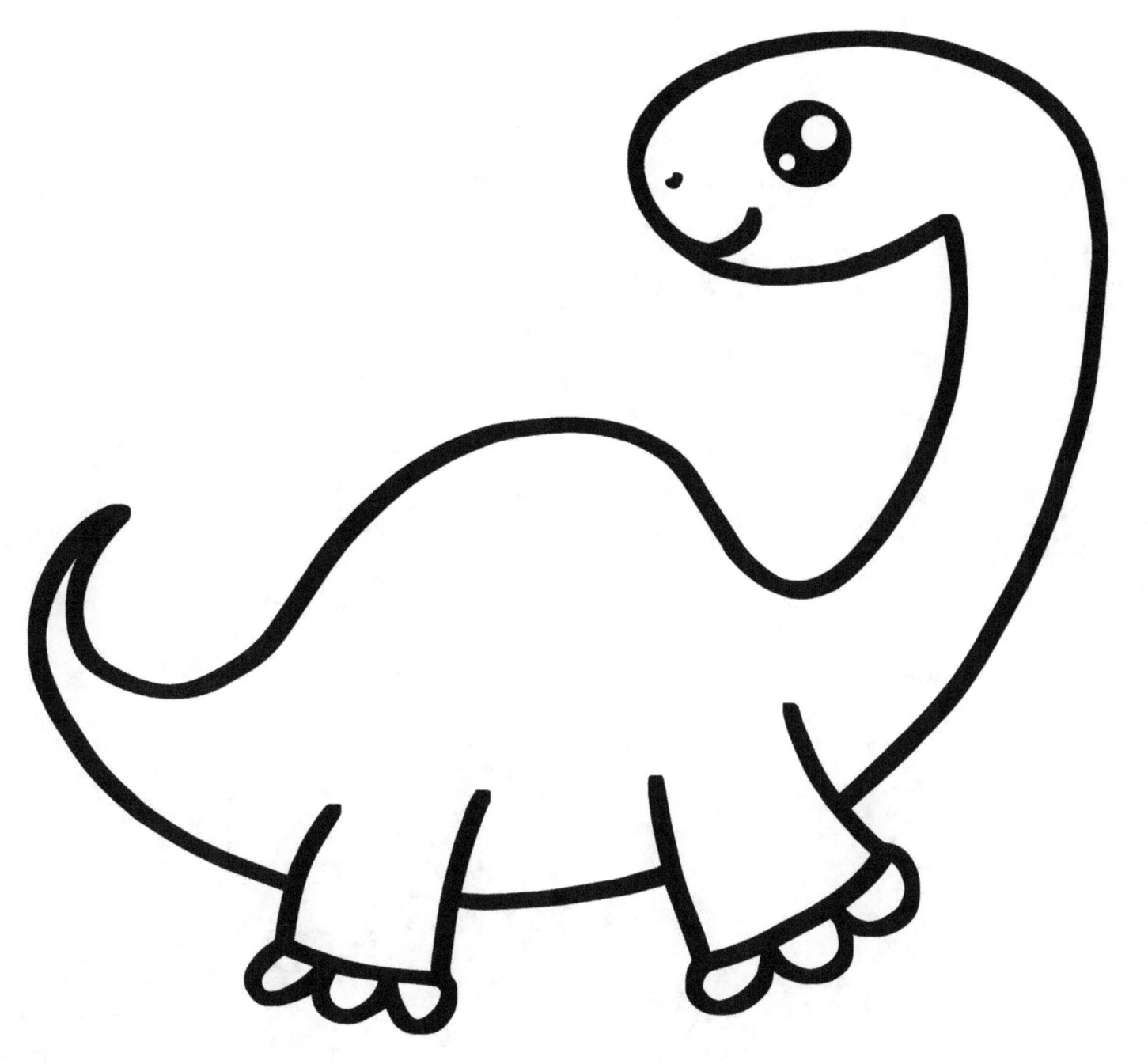

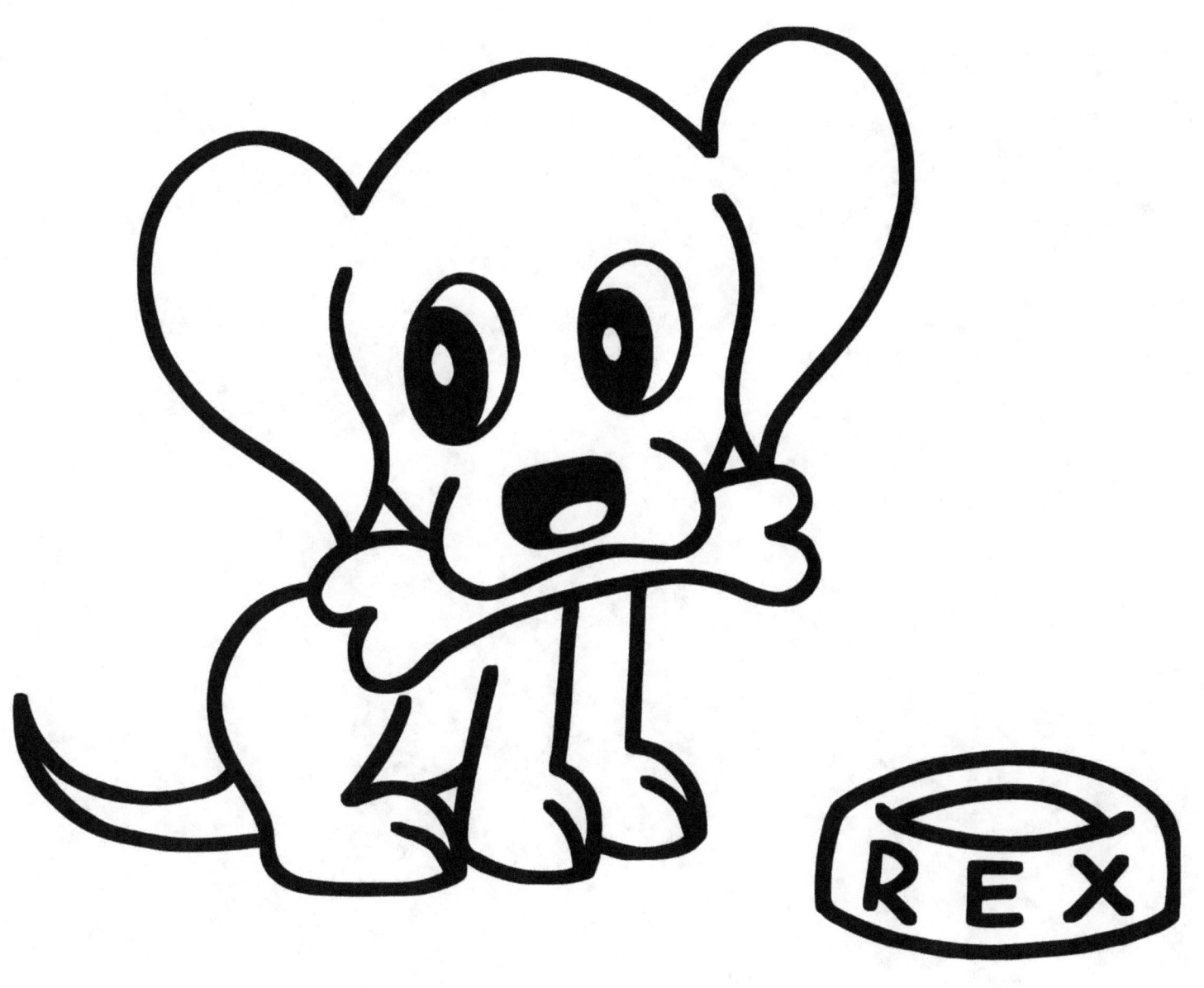

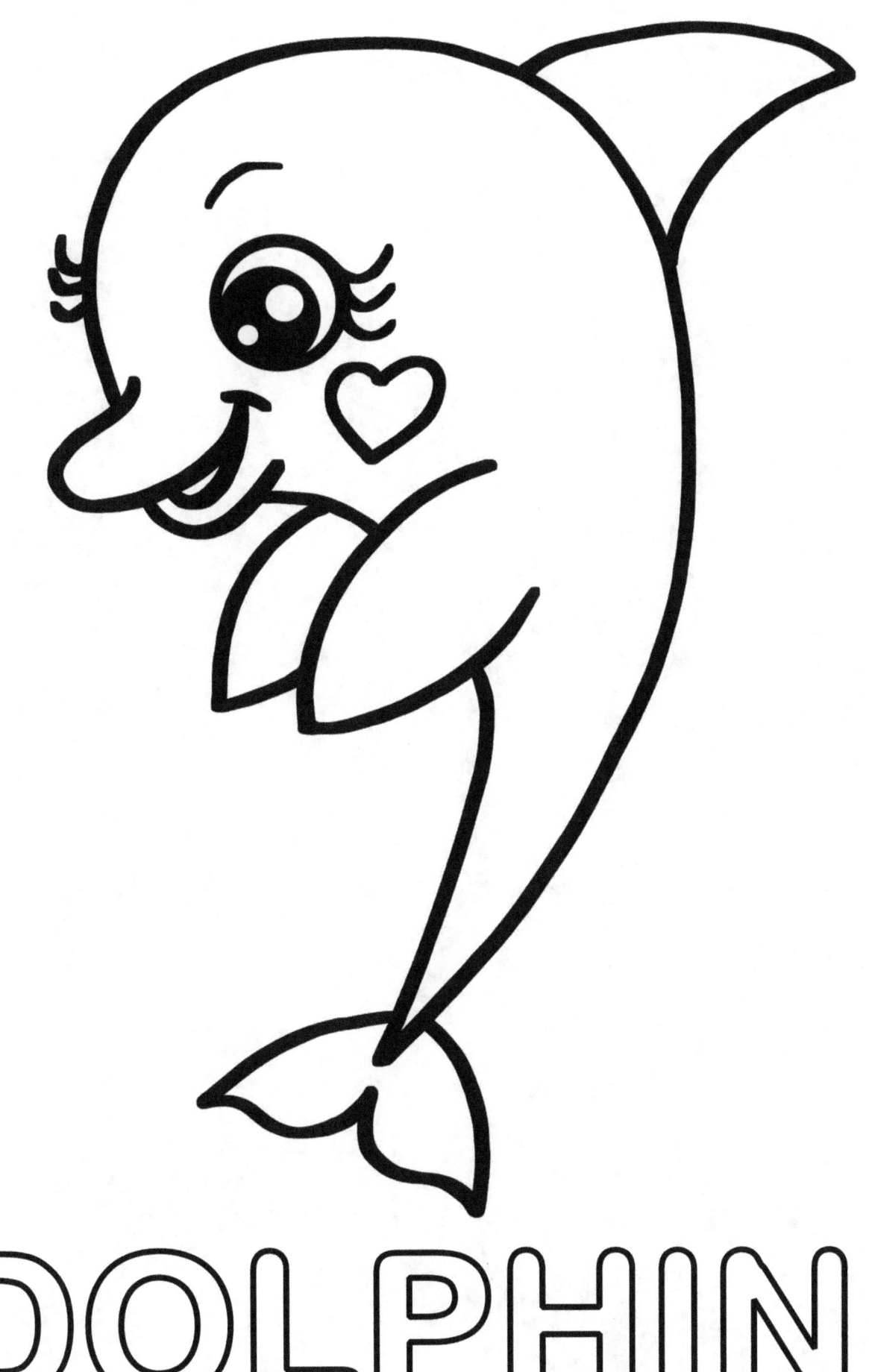

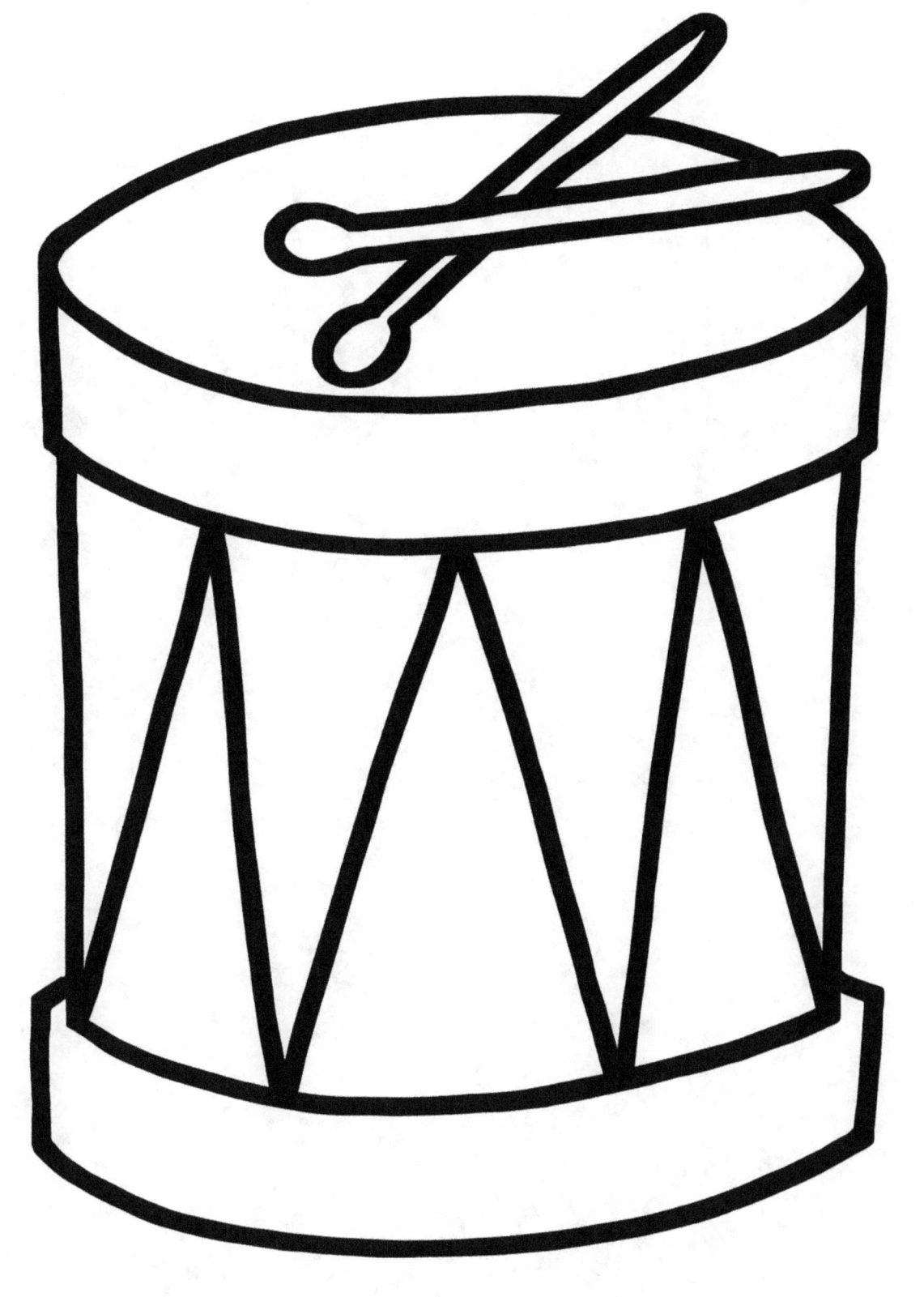

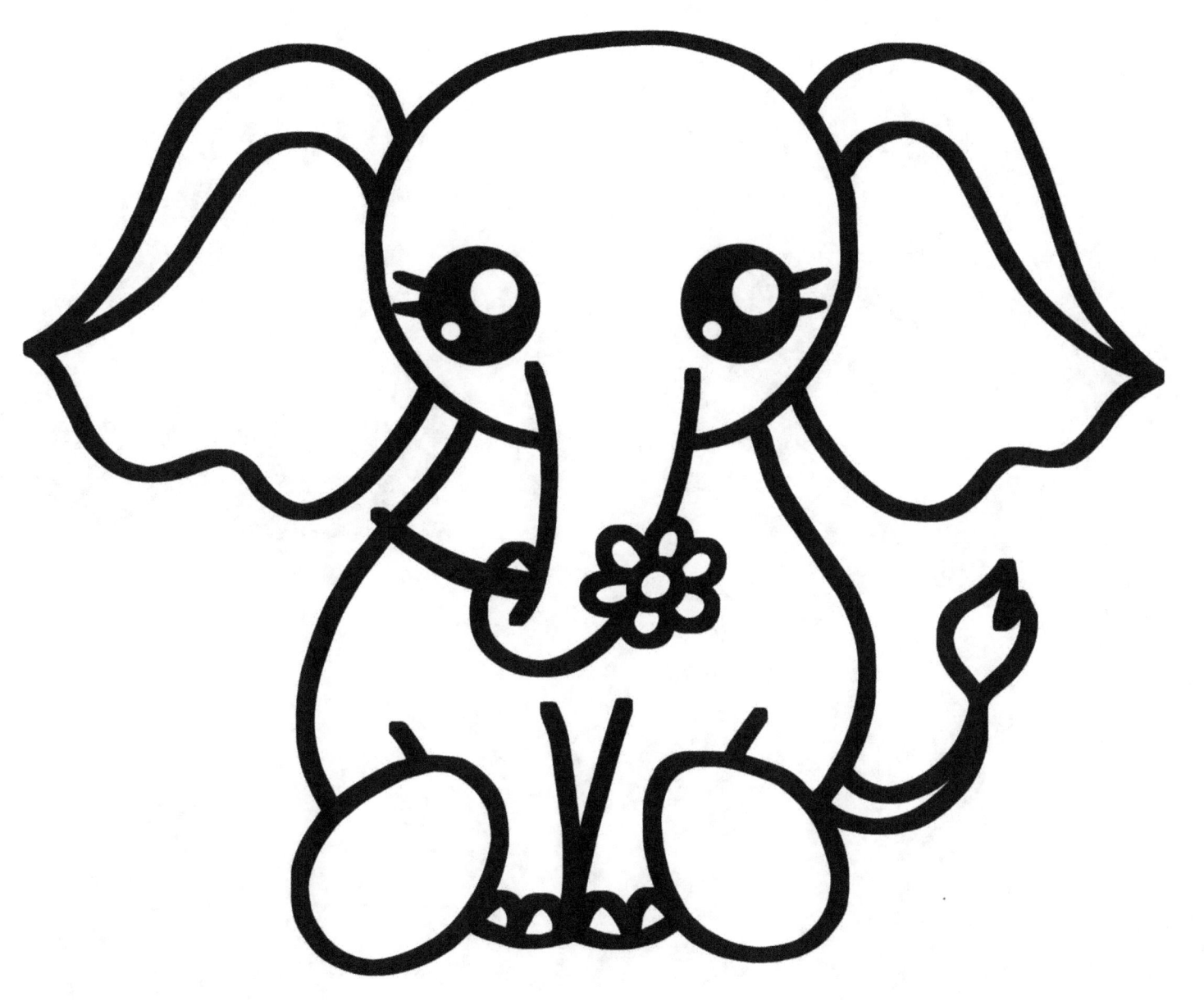

ELEPHANT

ELEPHANT

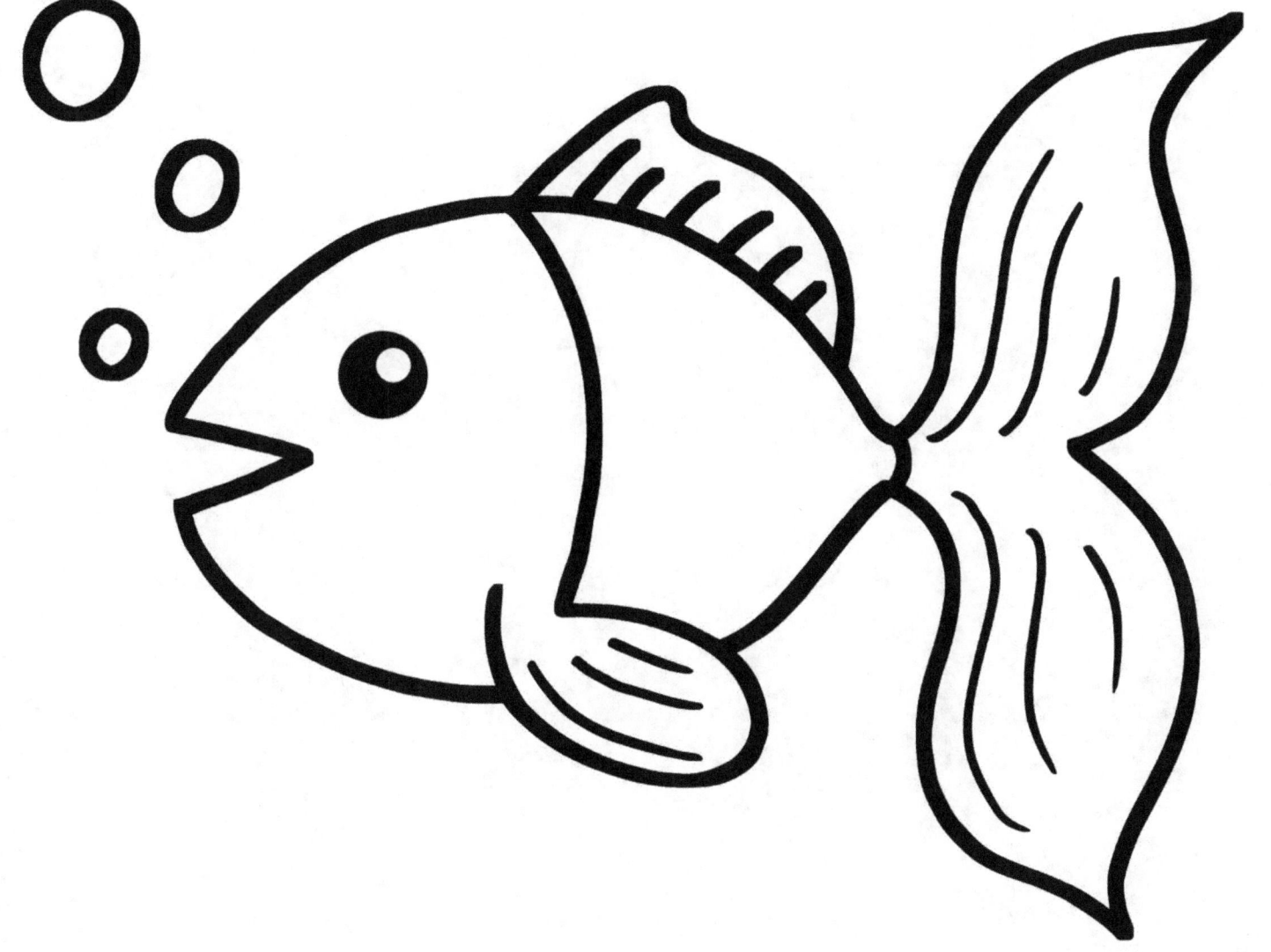

FISH

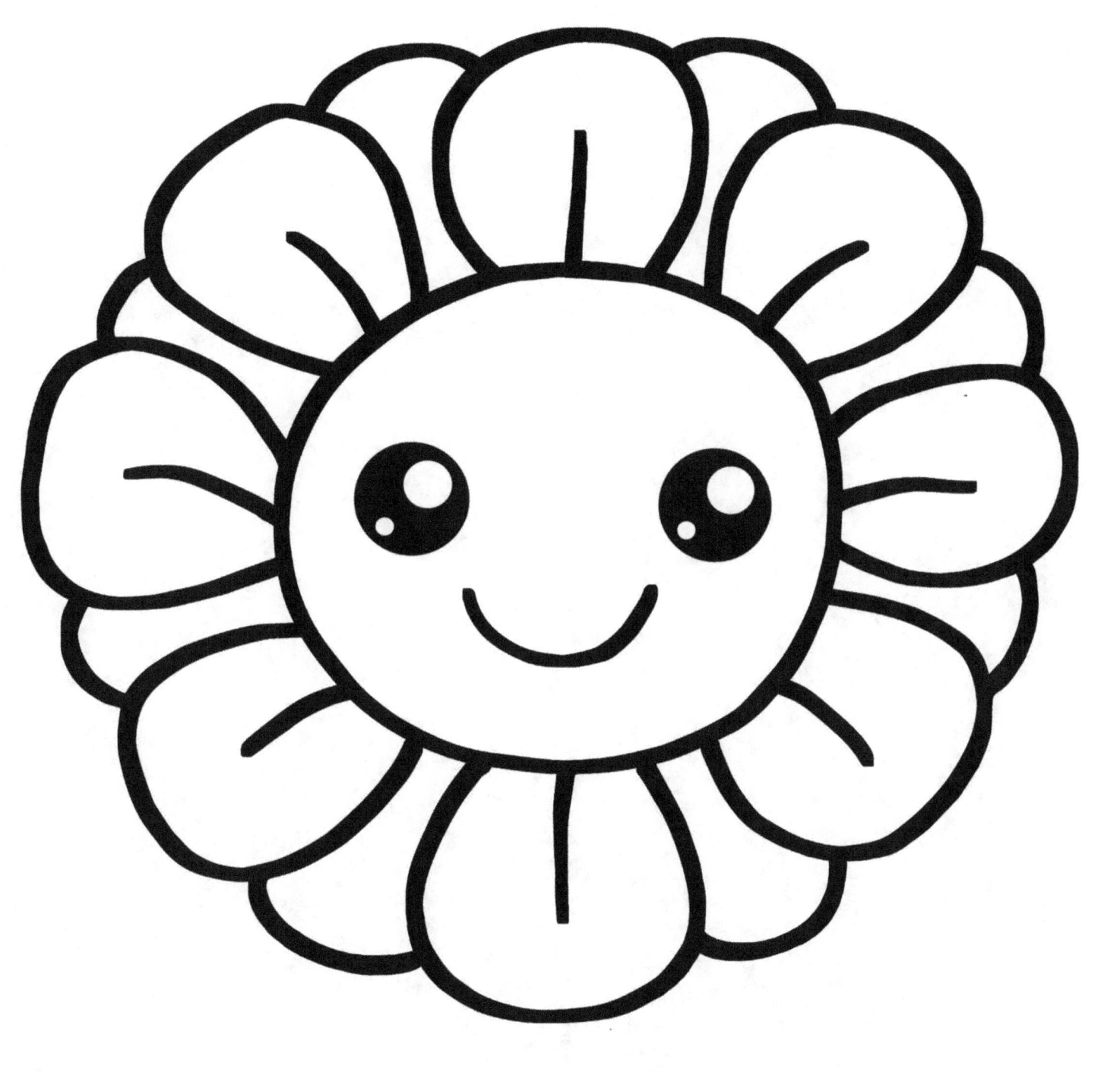

FLOWER

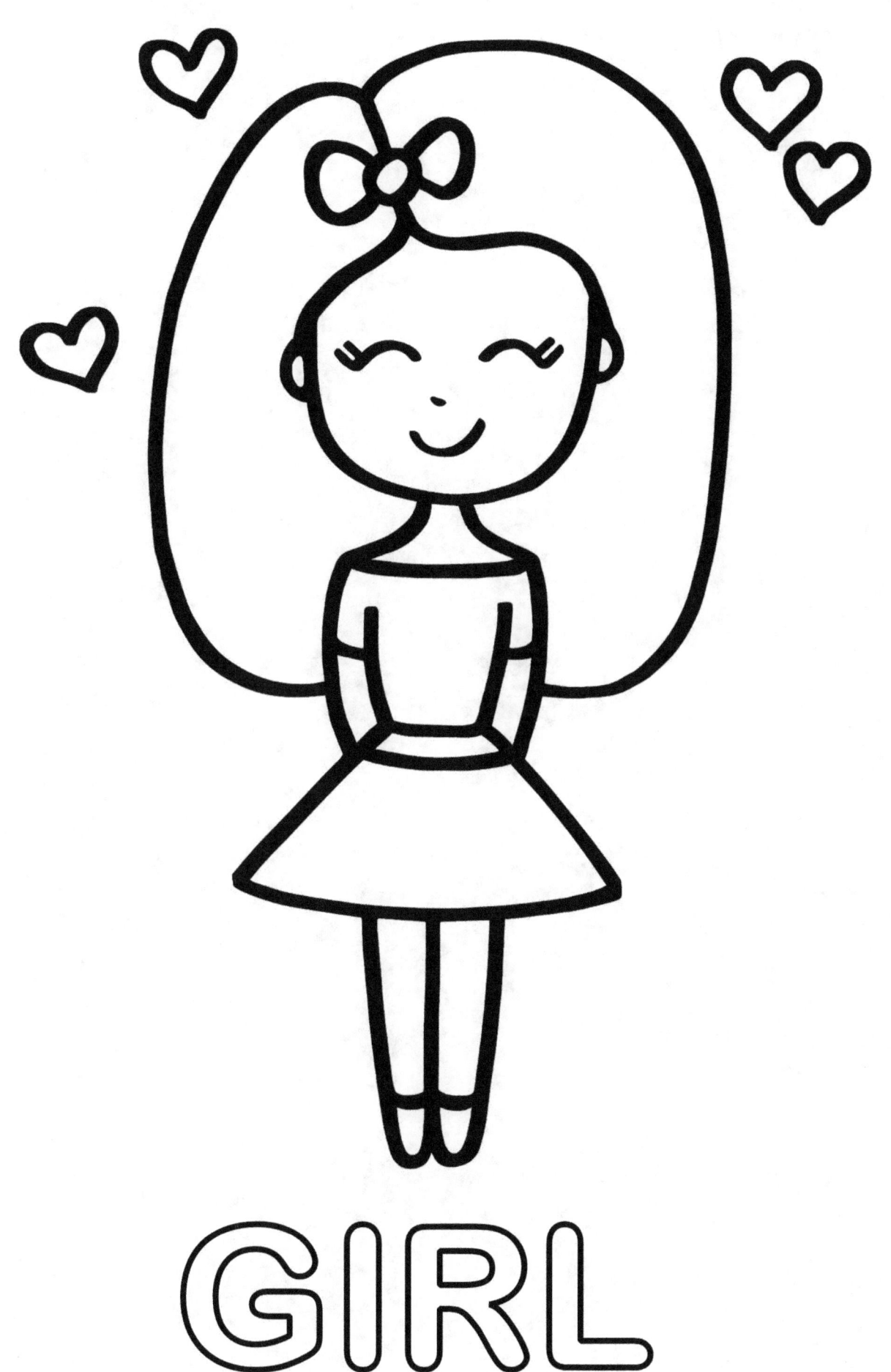

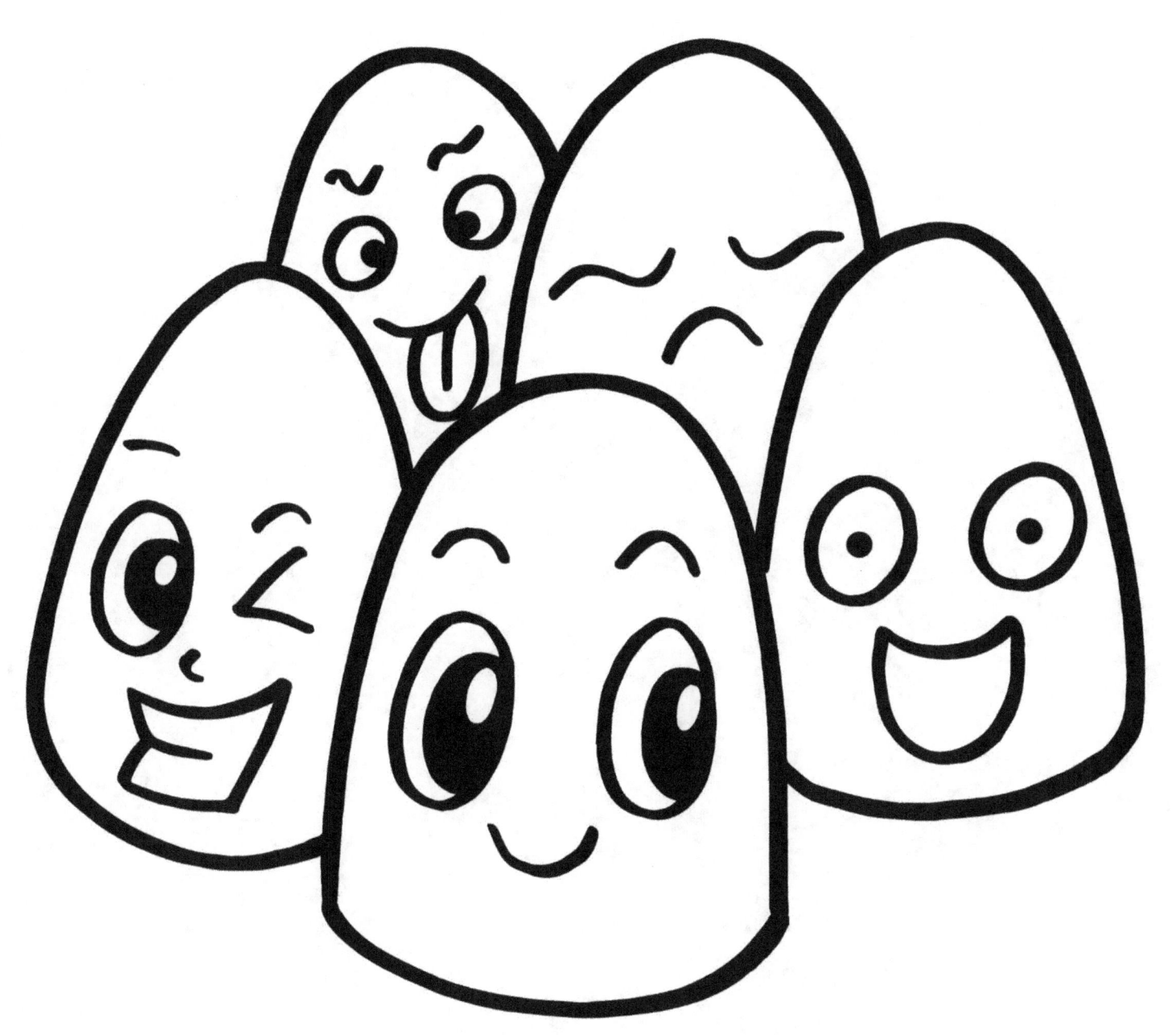

GUMDROPS

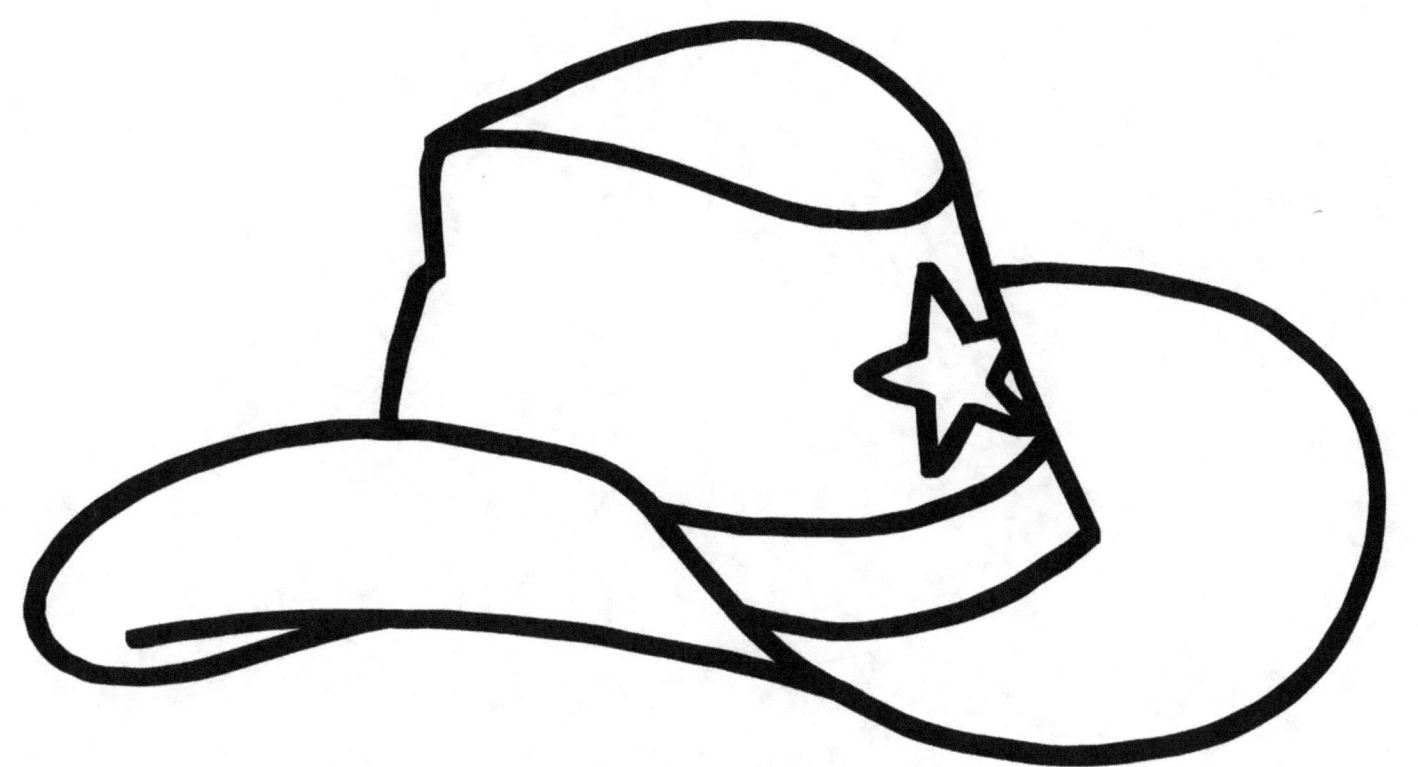

HAT

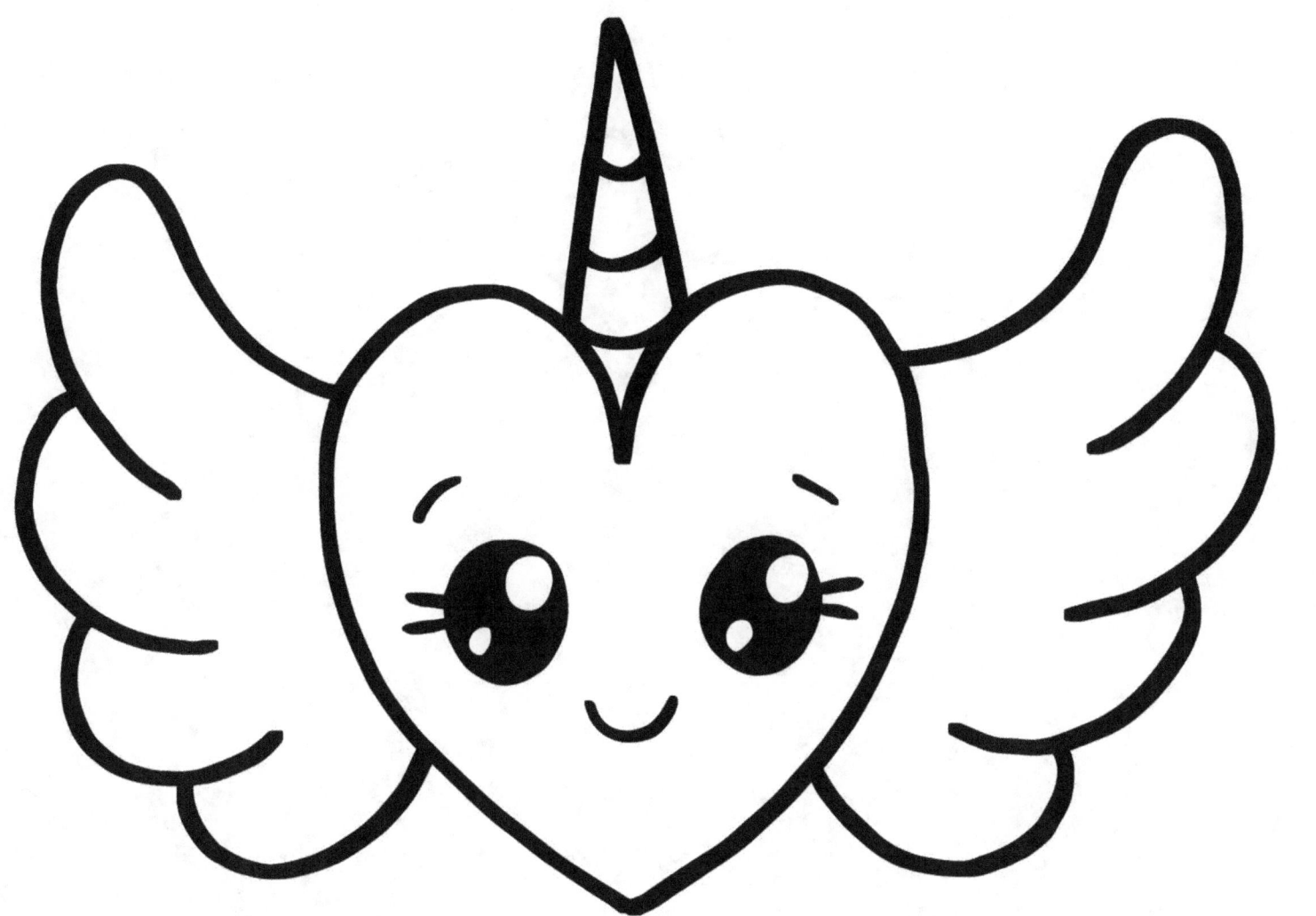

HEART

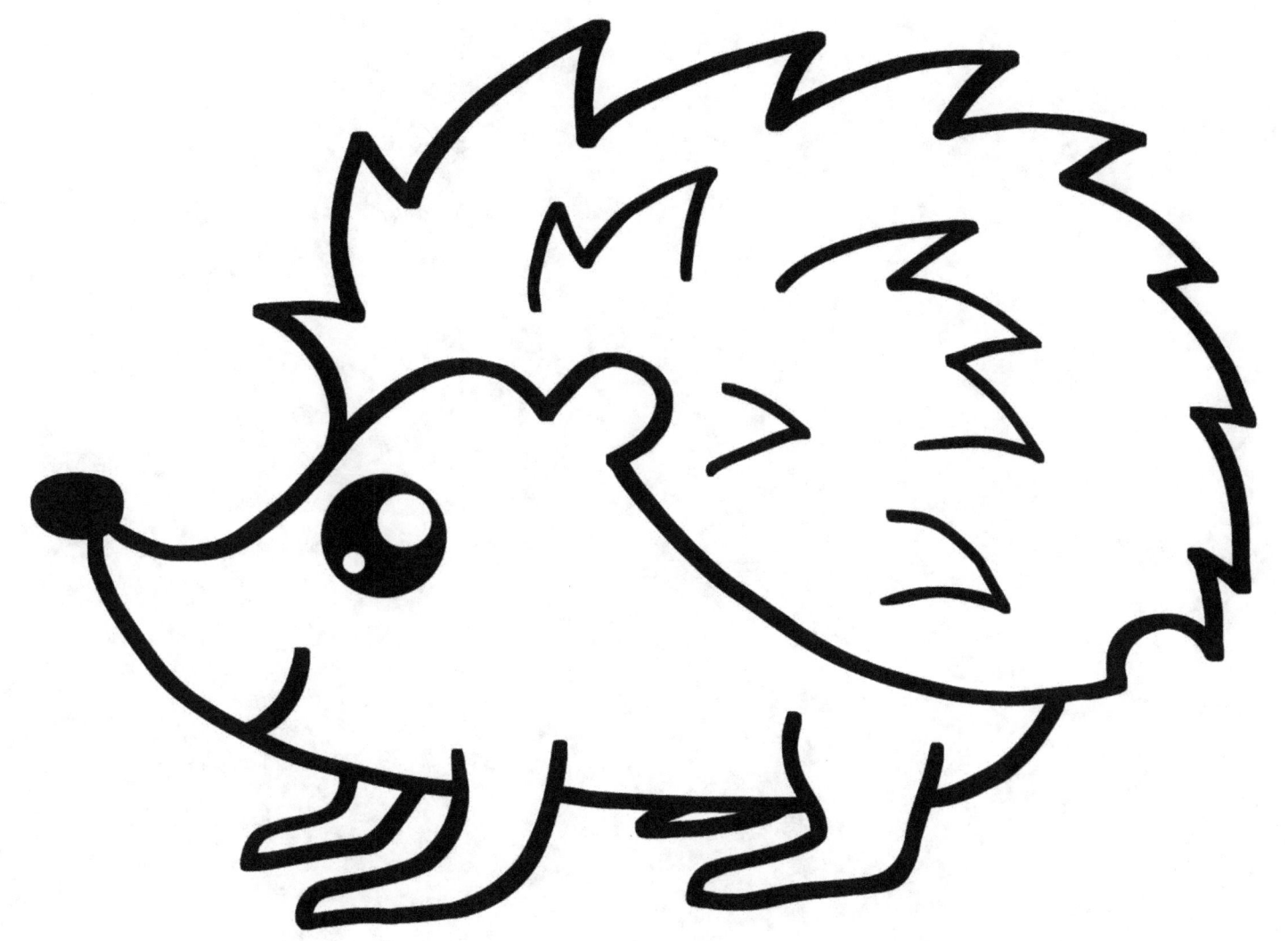

HEDGEHOG

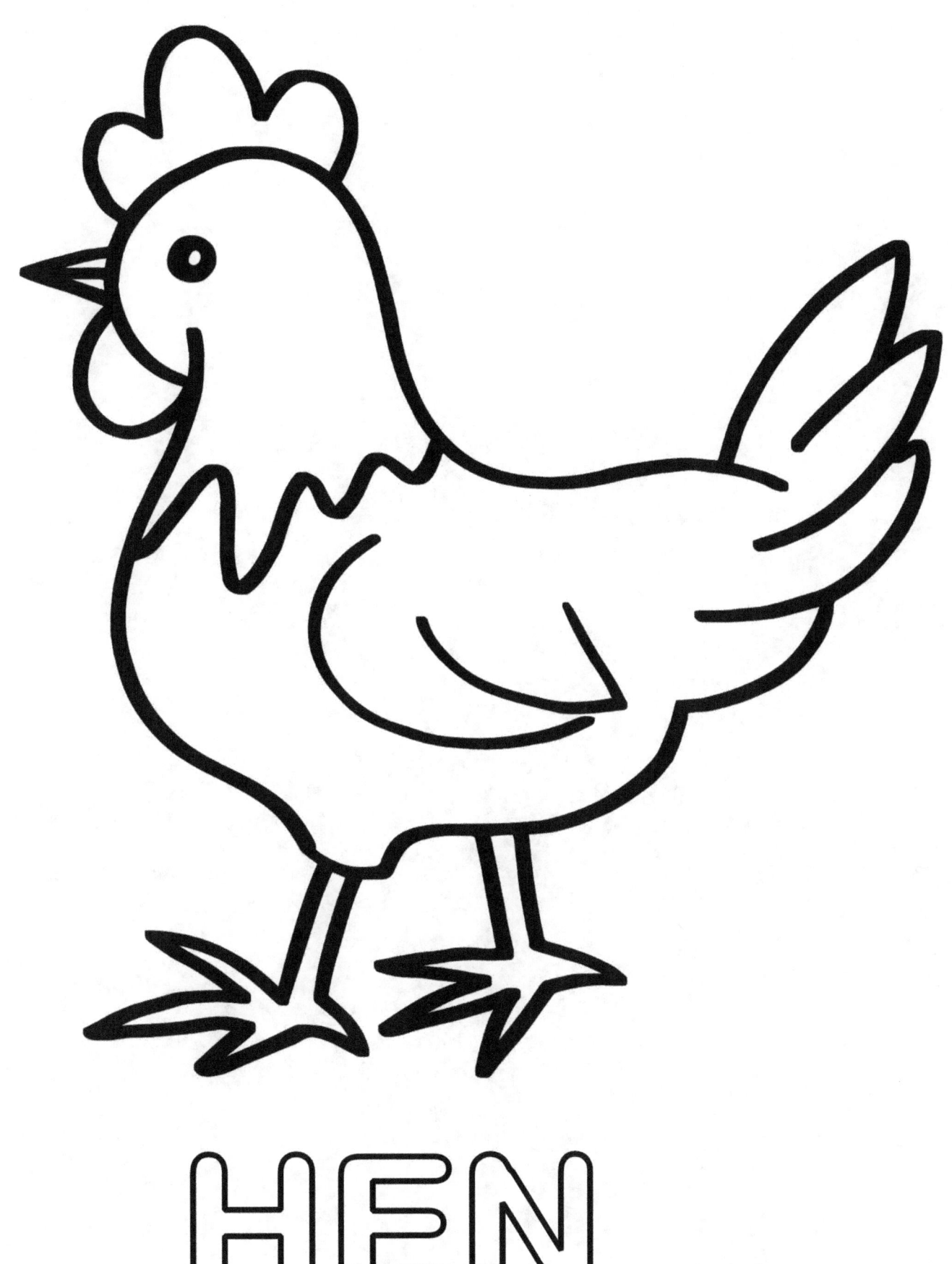

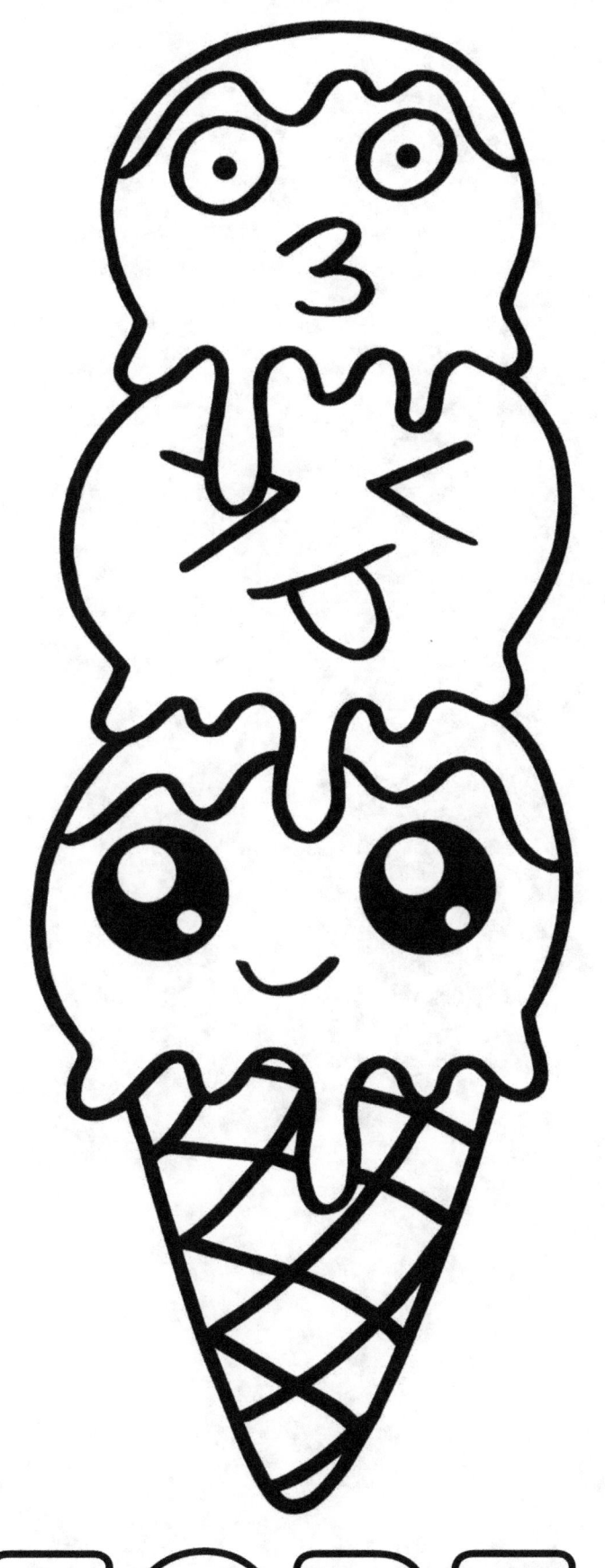

ICECREAM

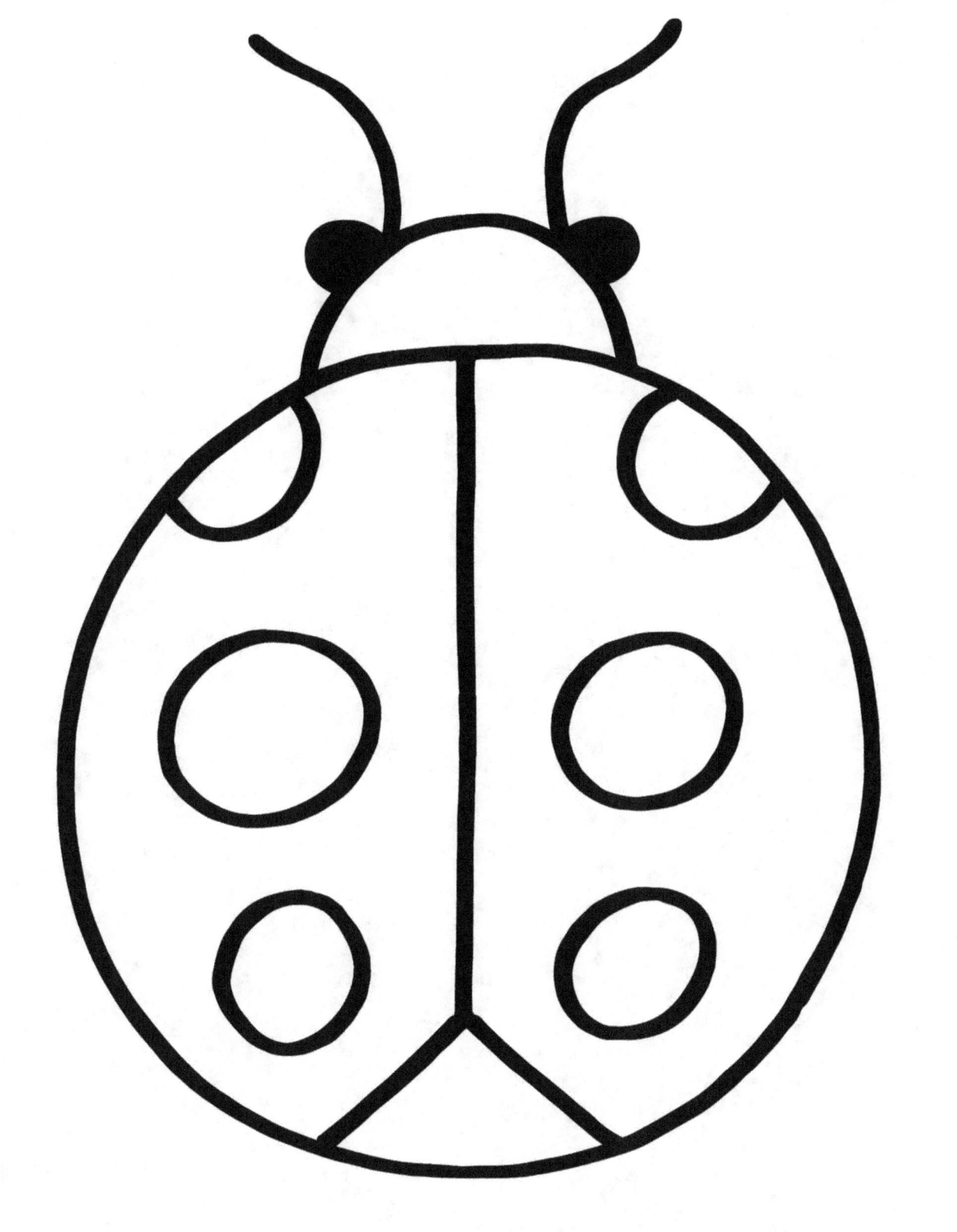

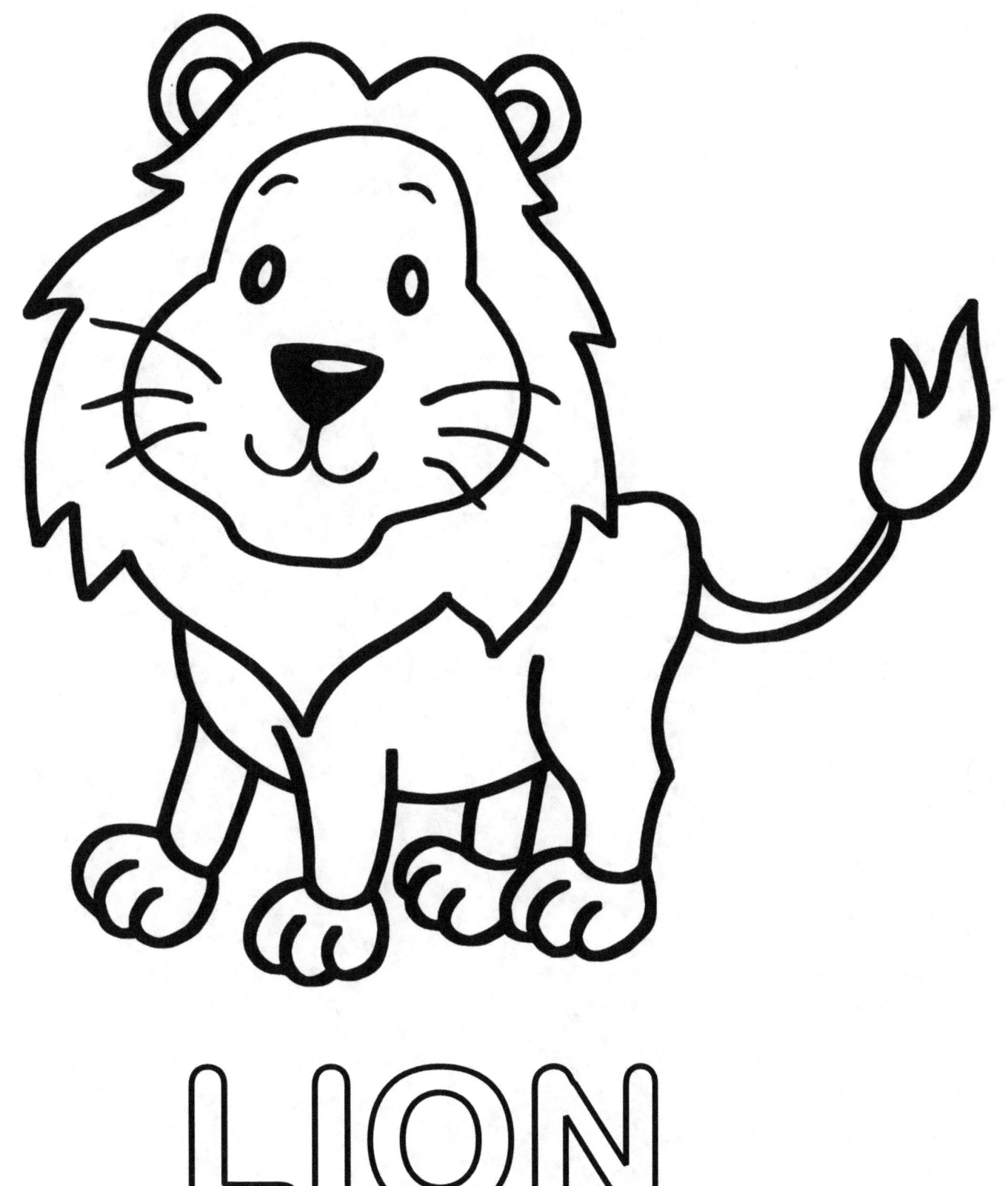

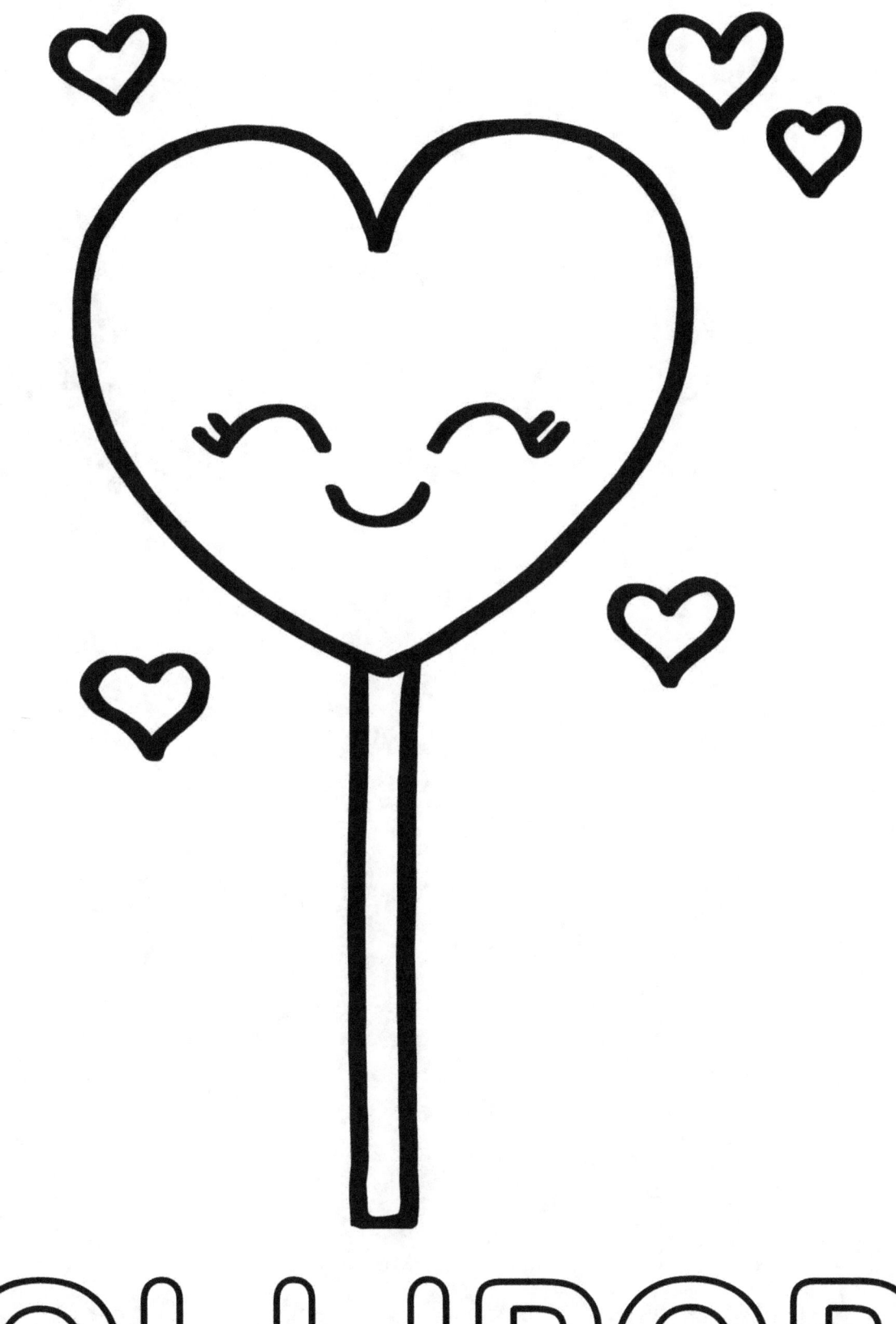

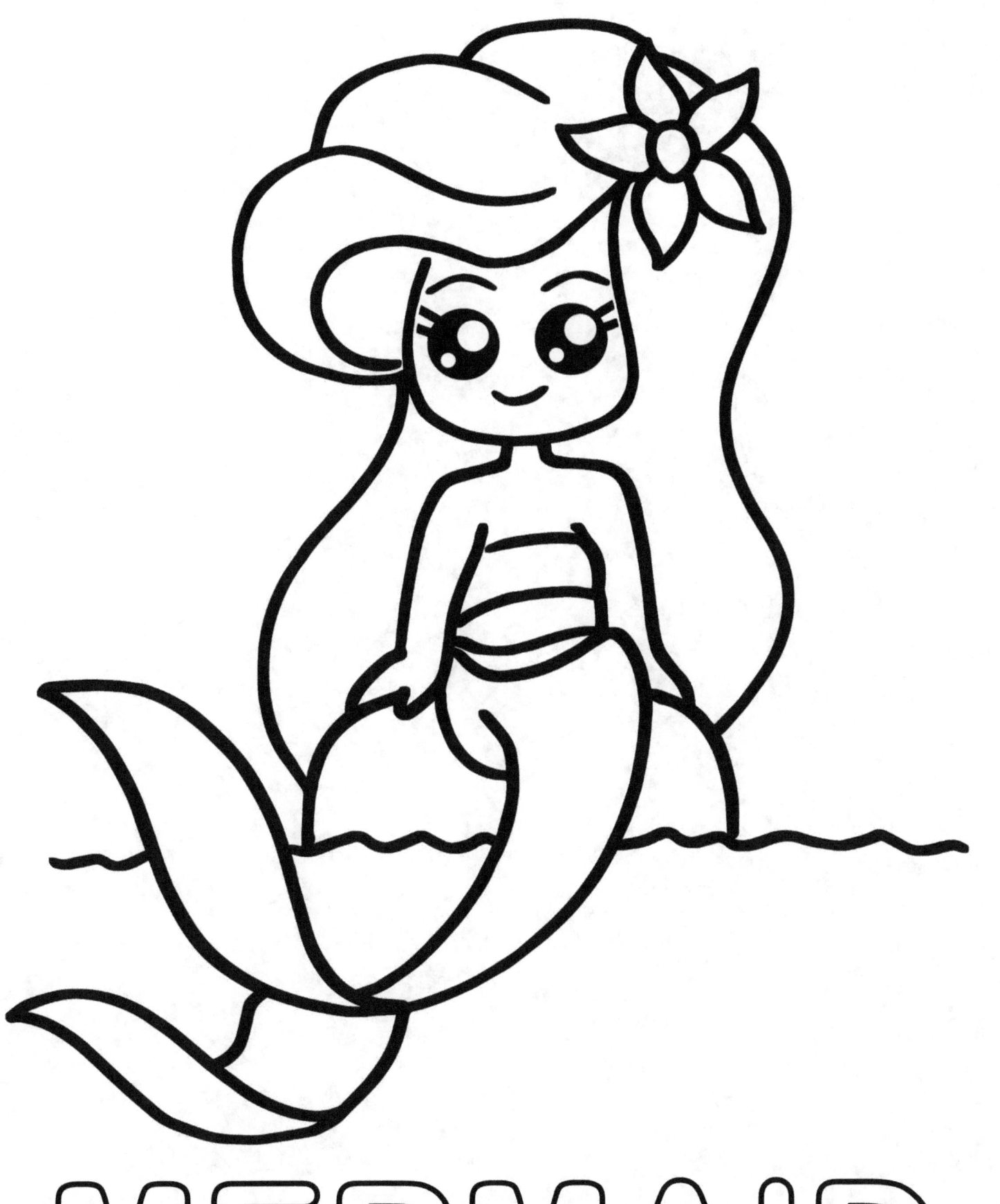

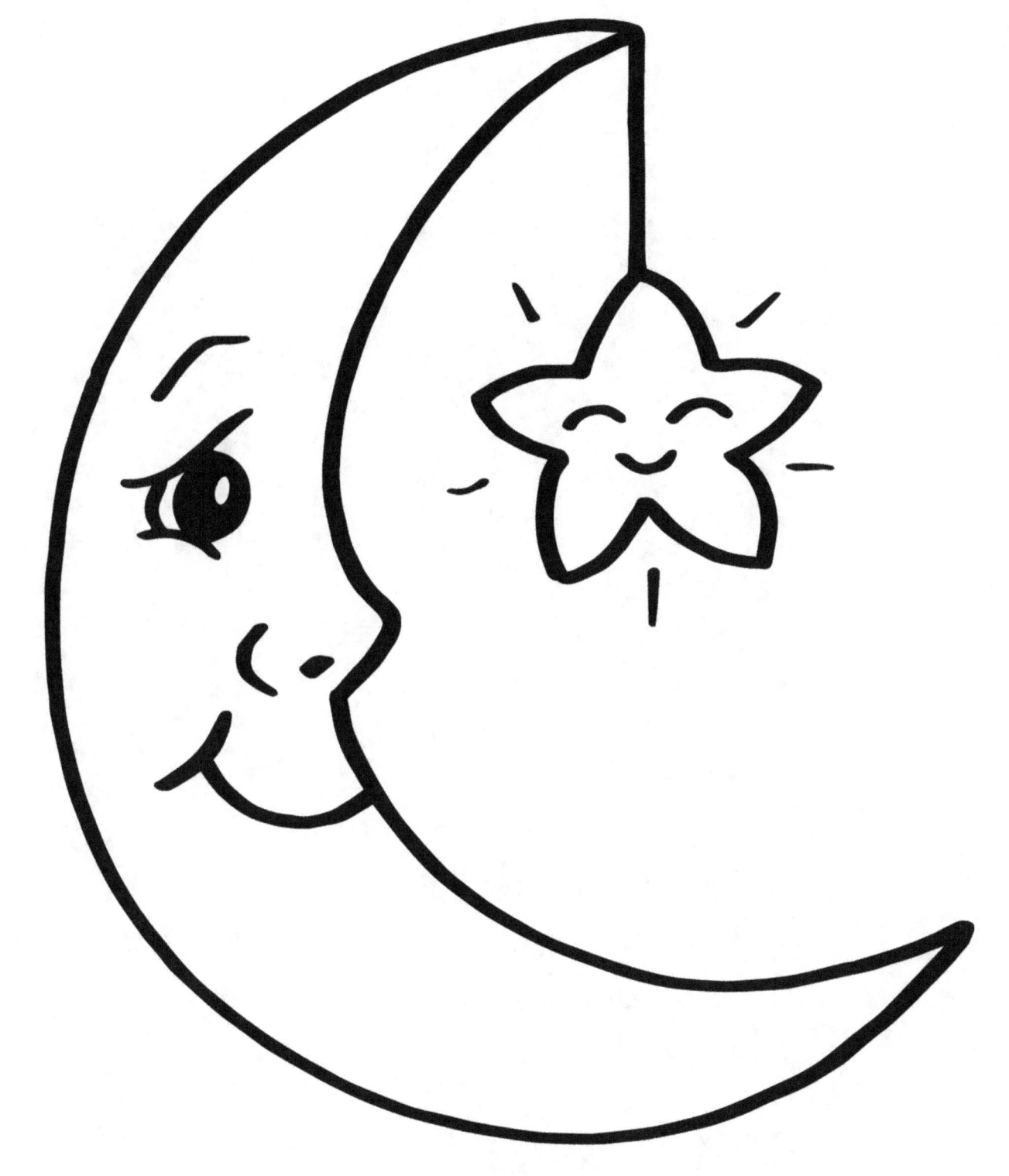

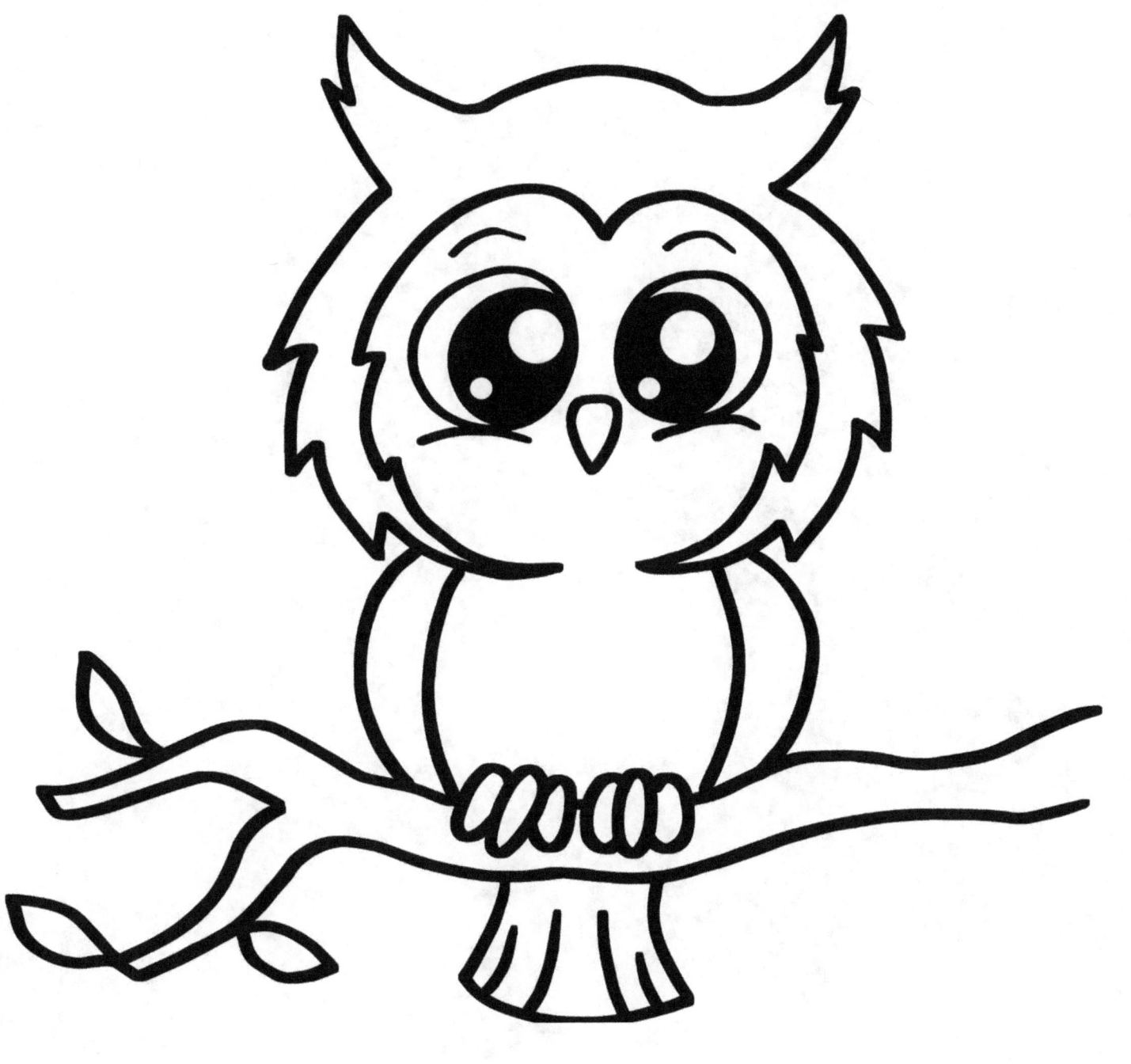

OWL

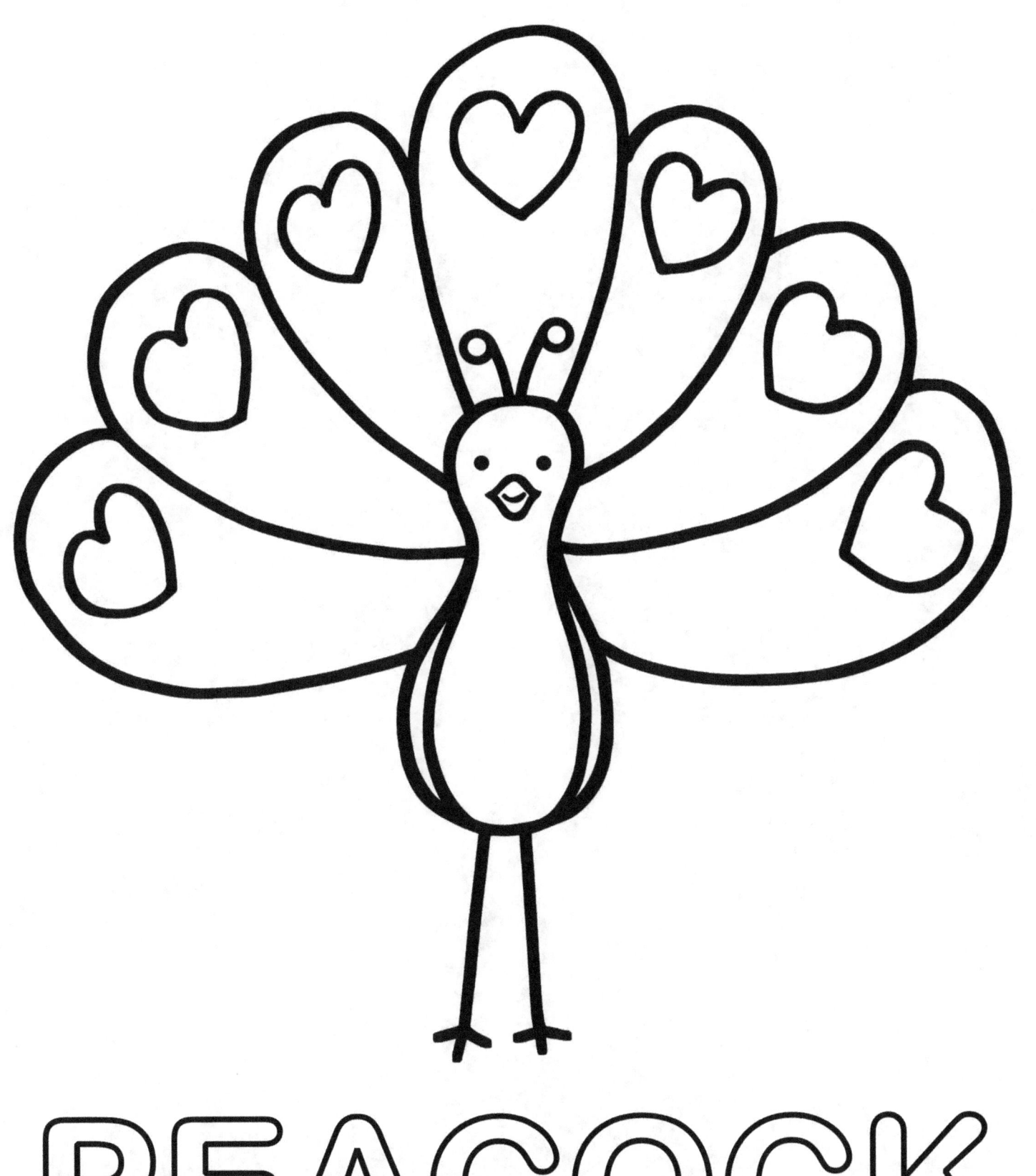

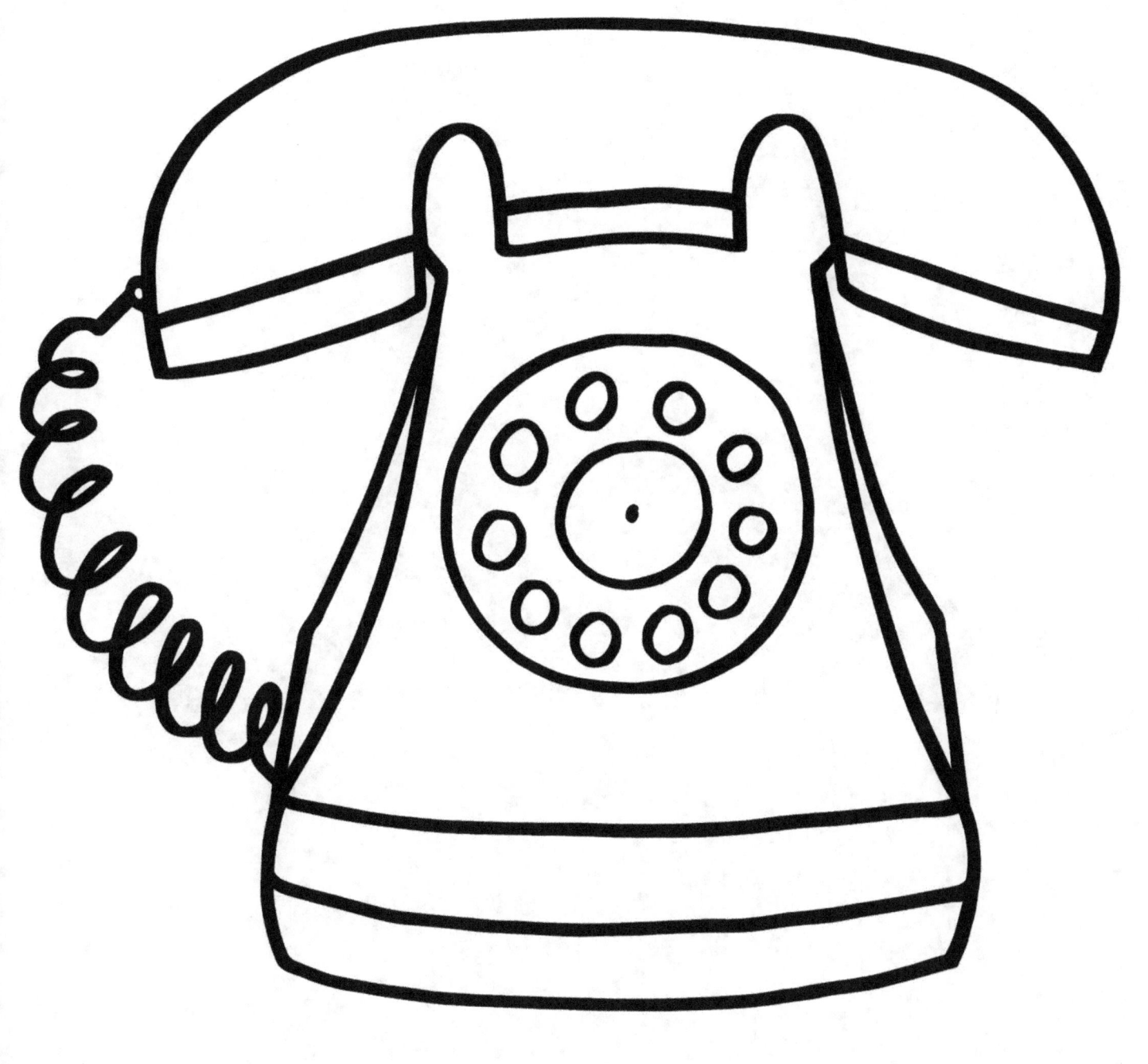

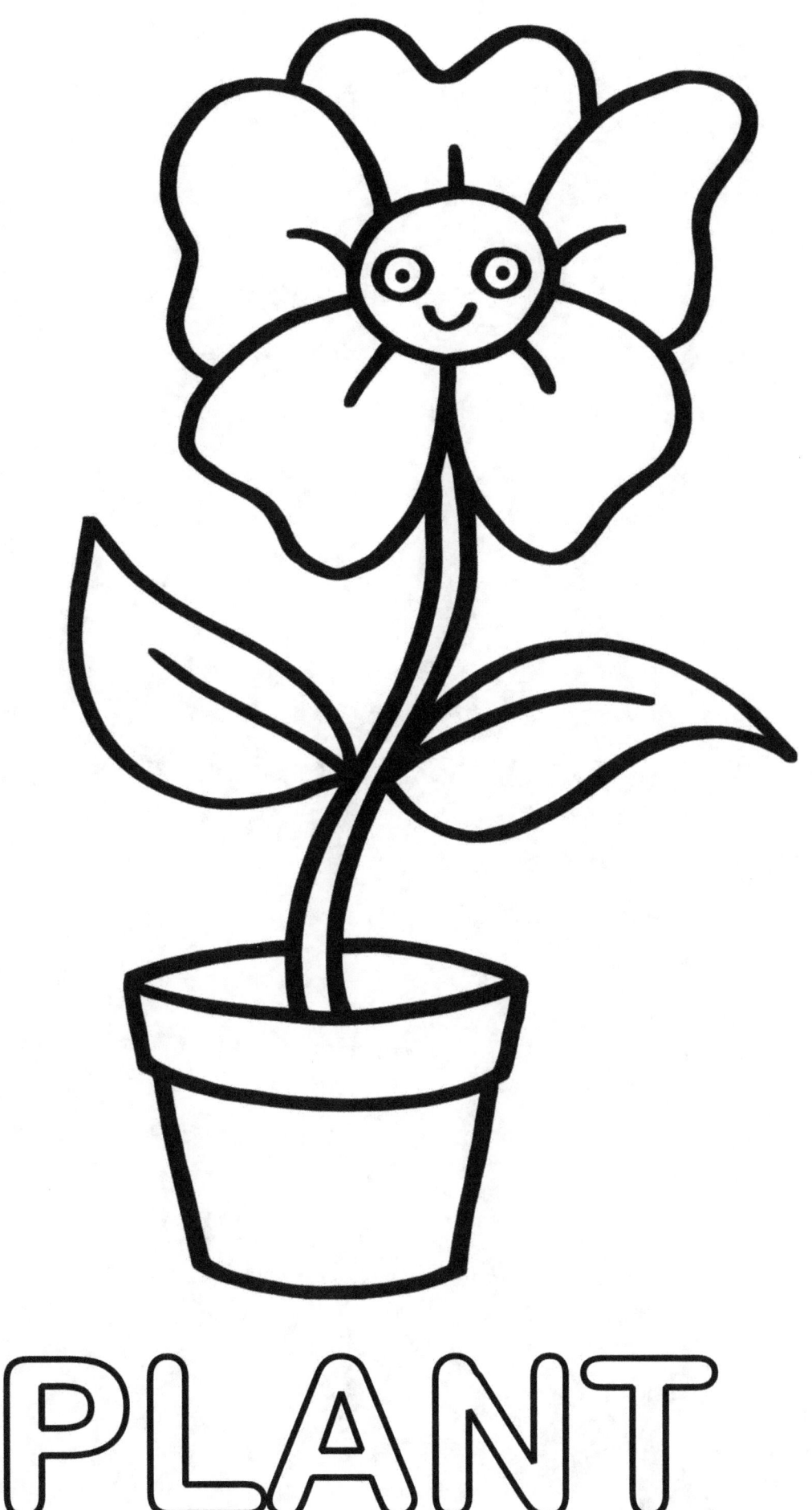

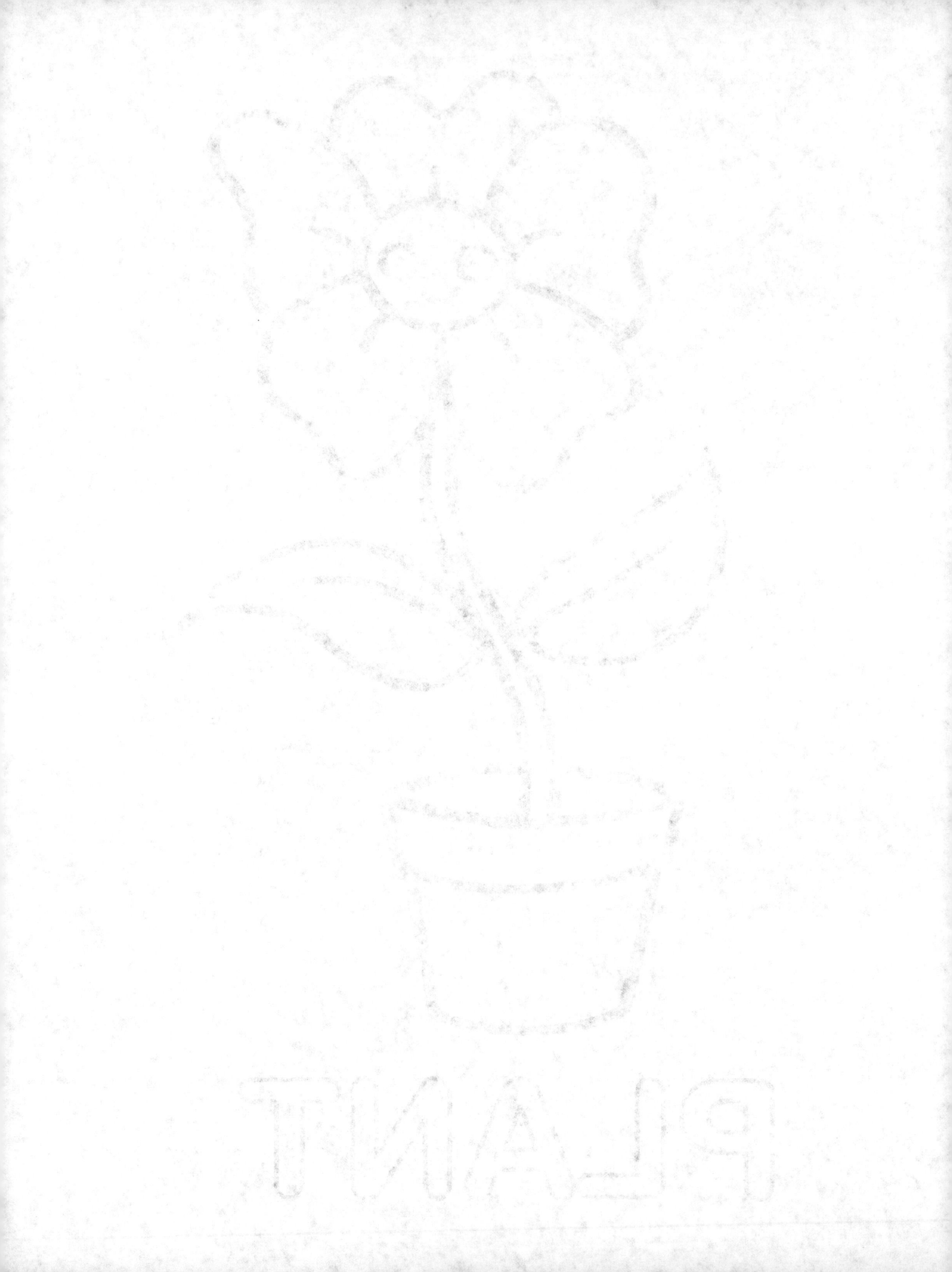

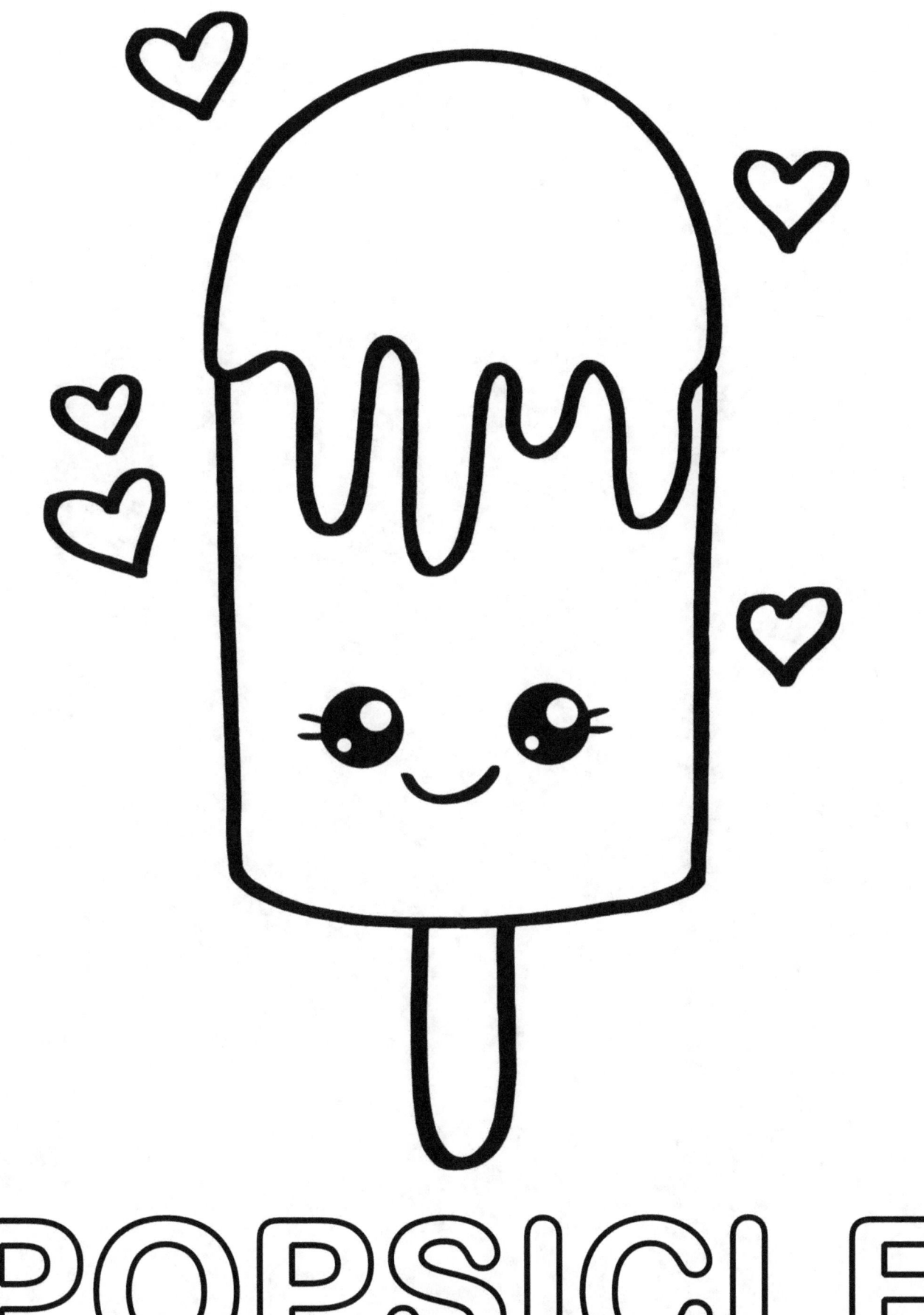

POPSICLE

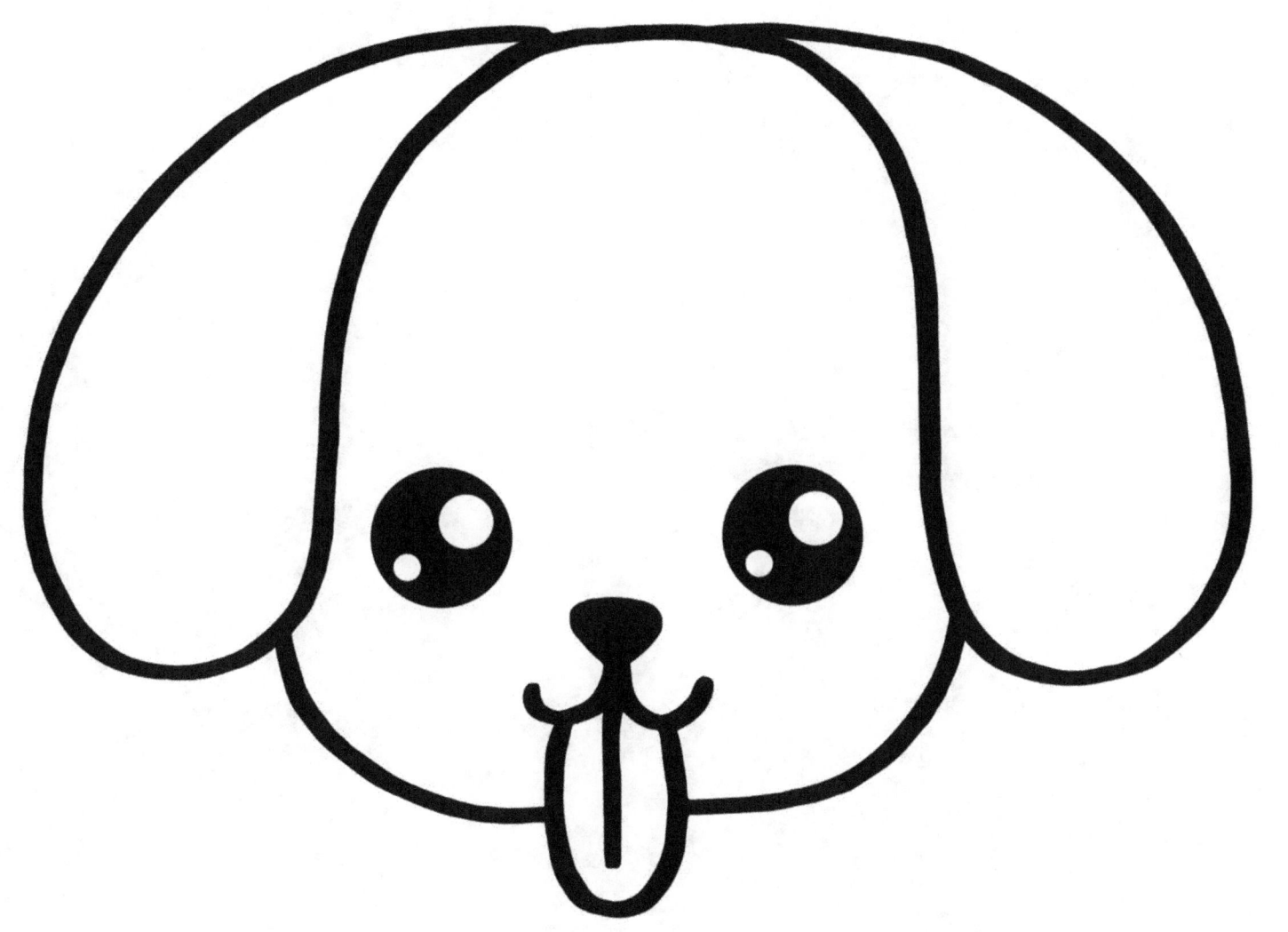

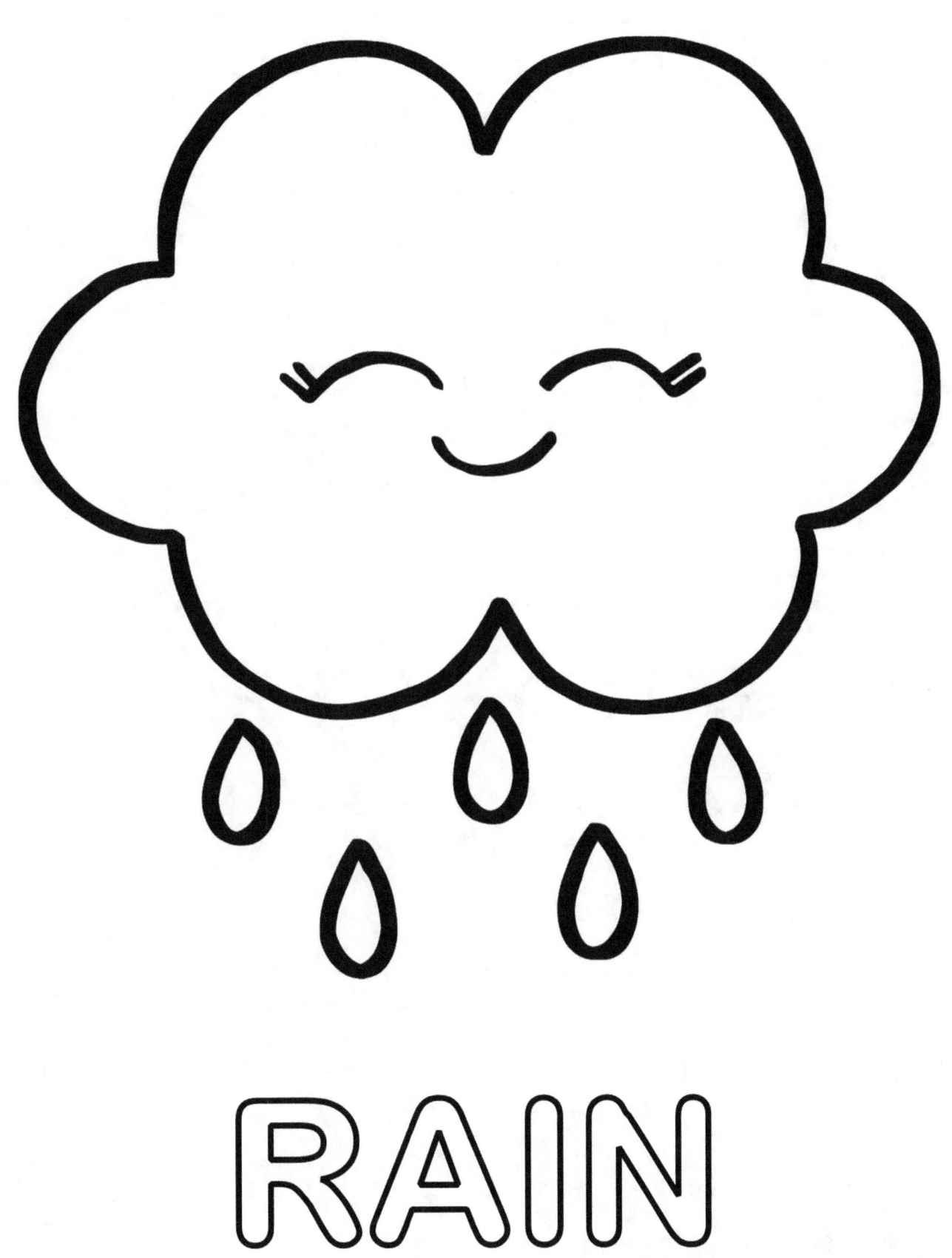

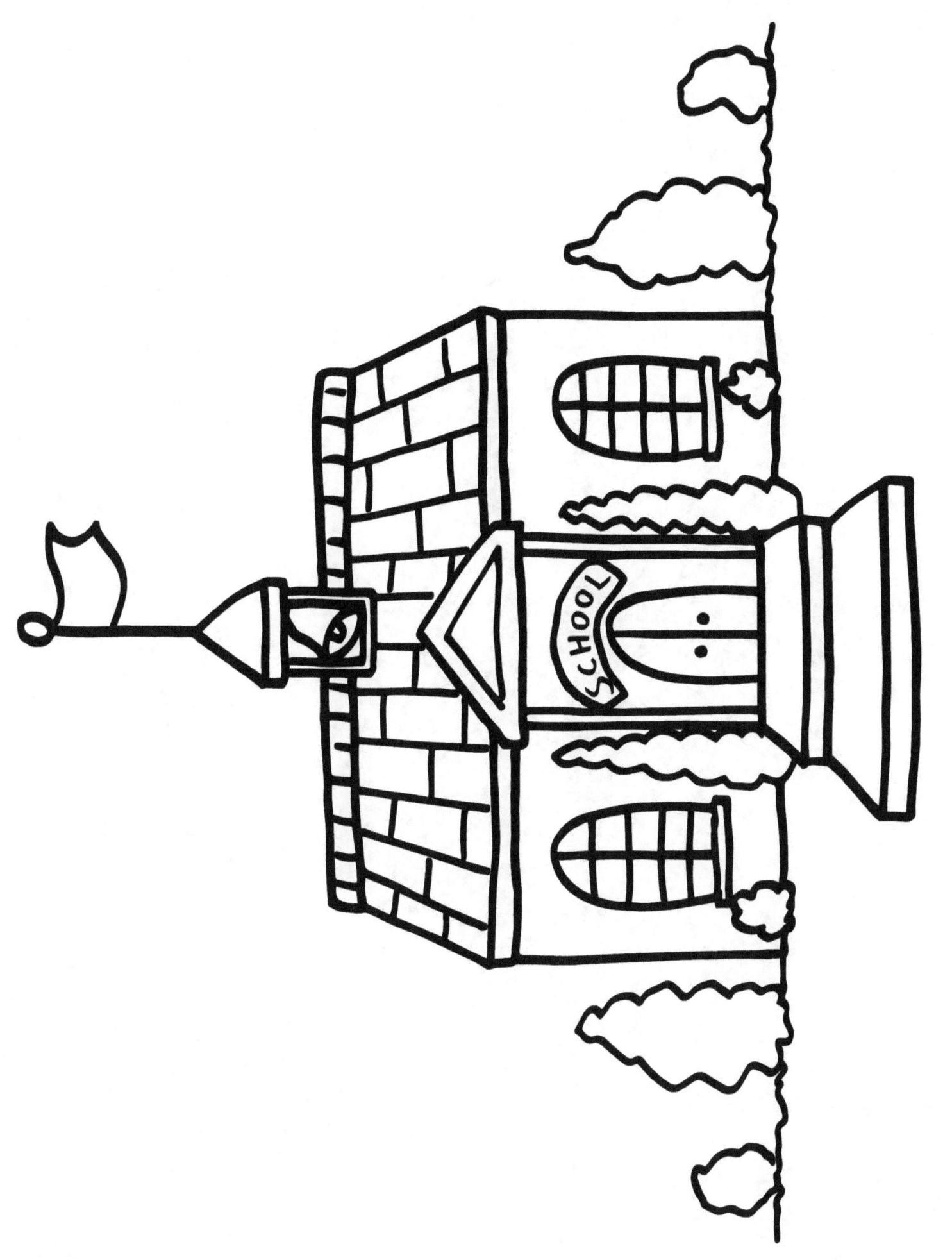

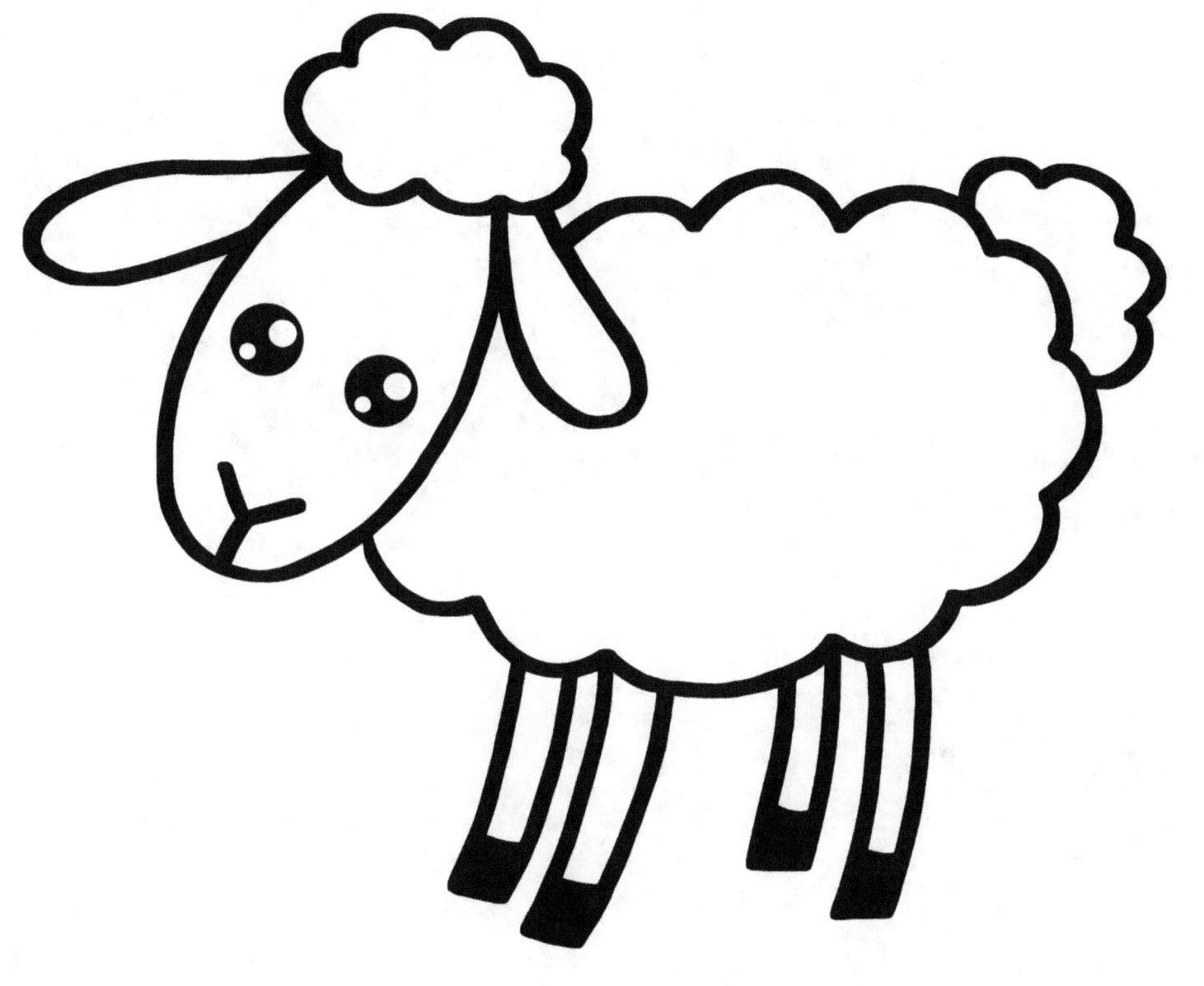

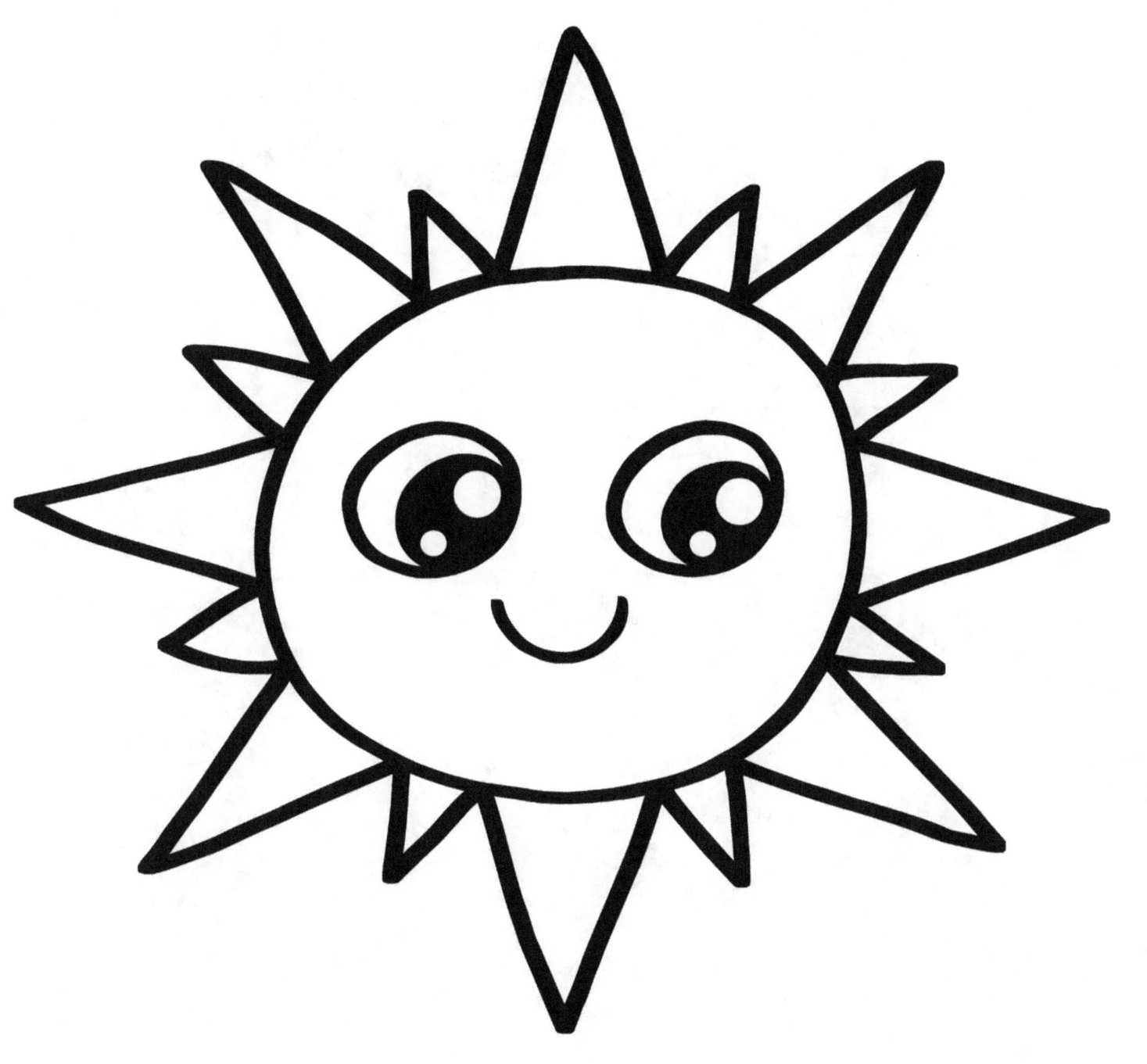

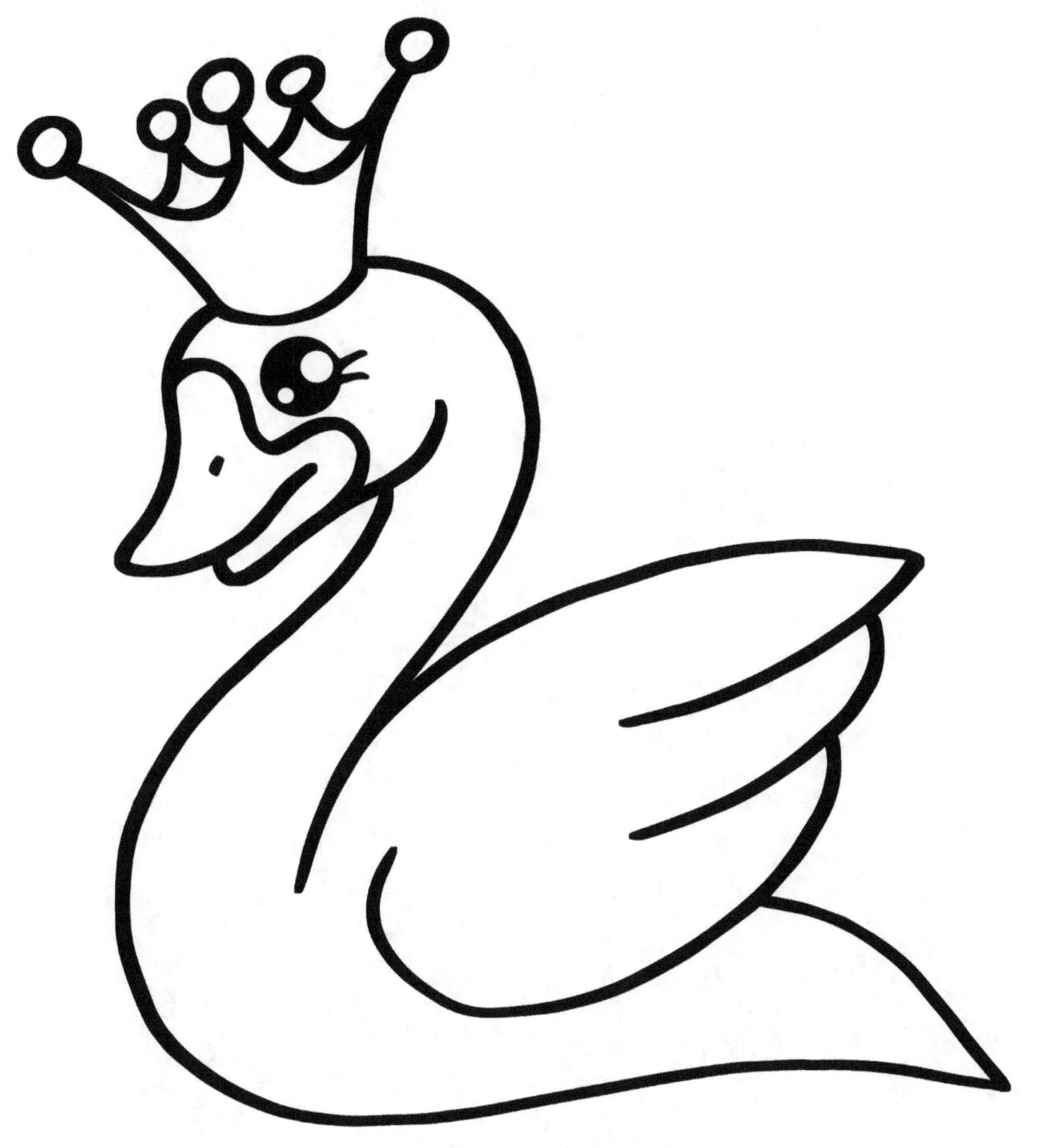

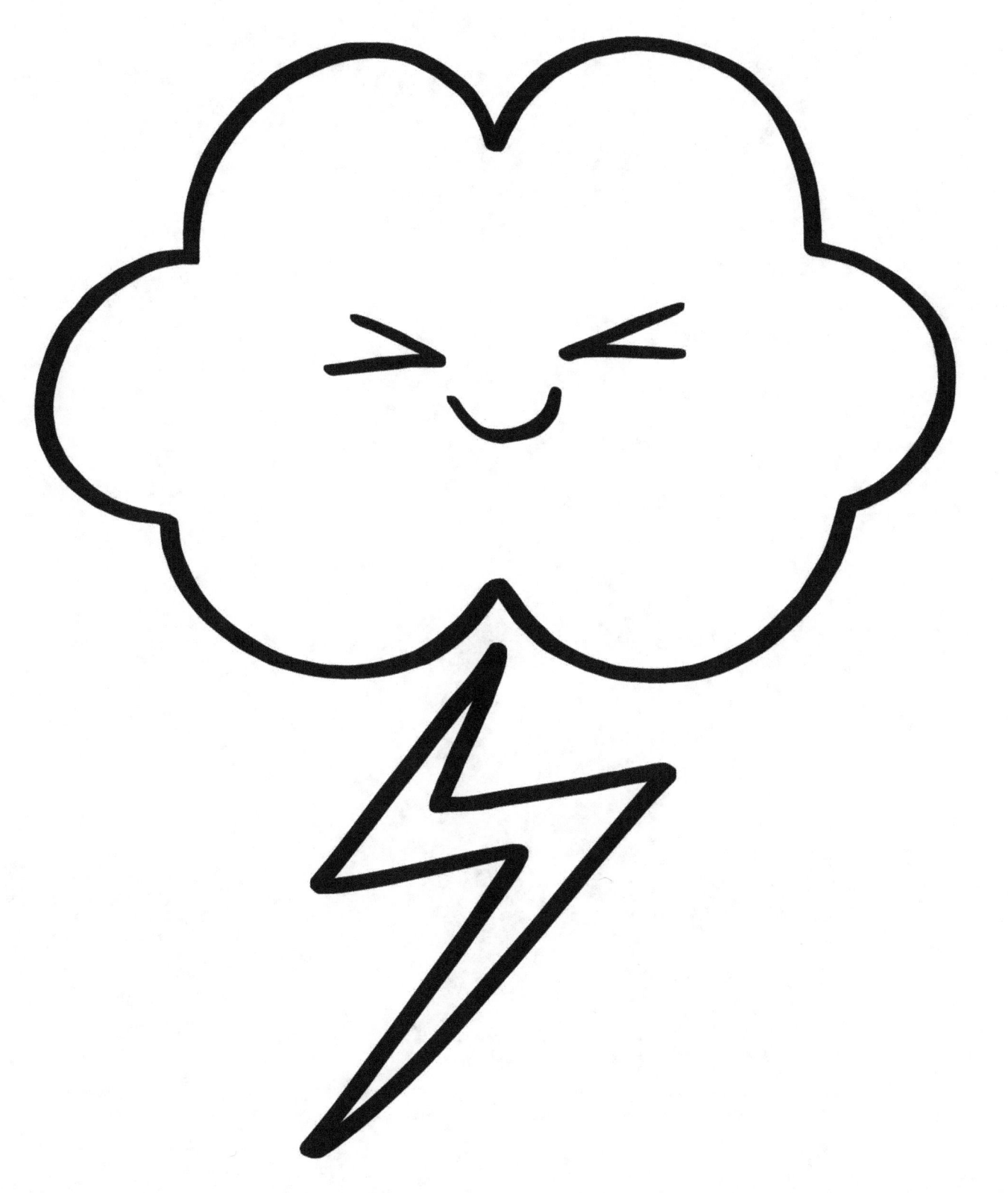

THUNDER

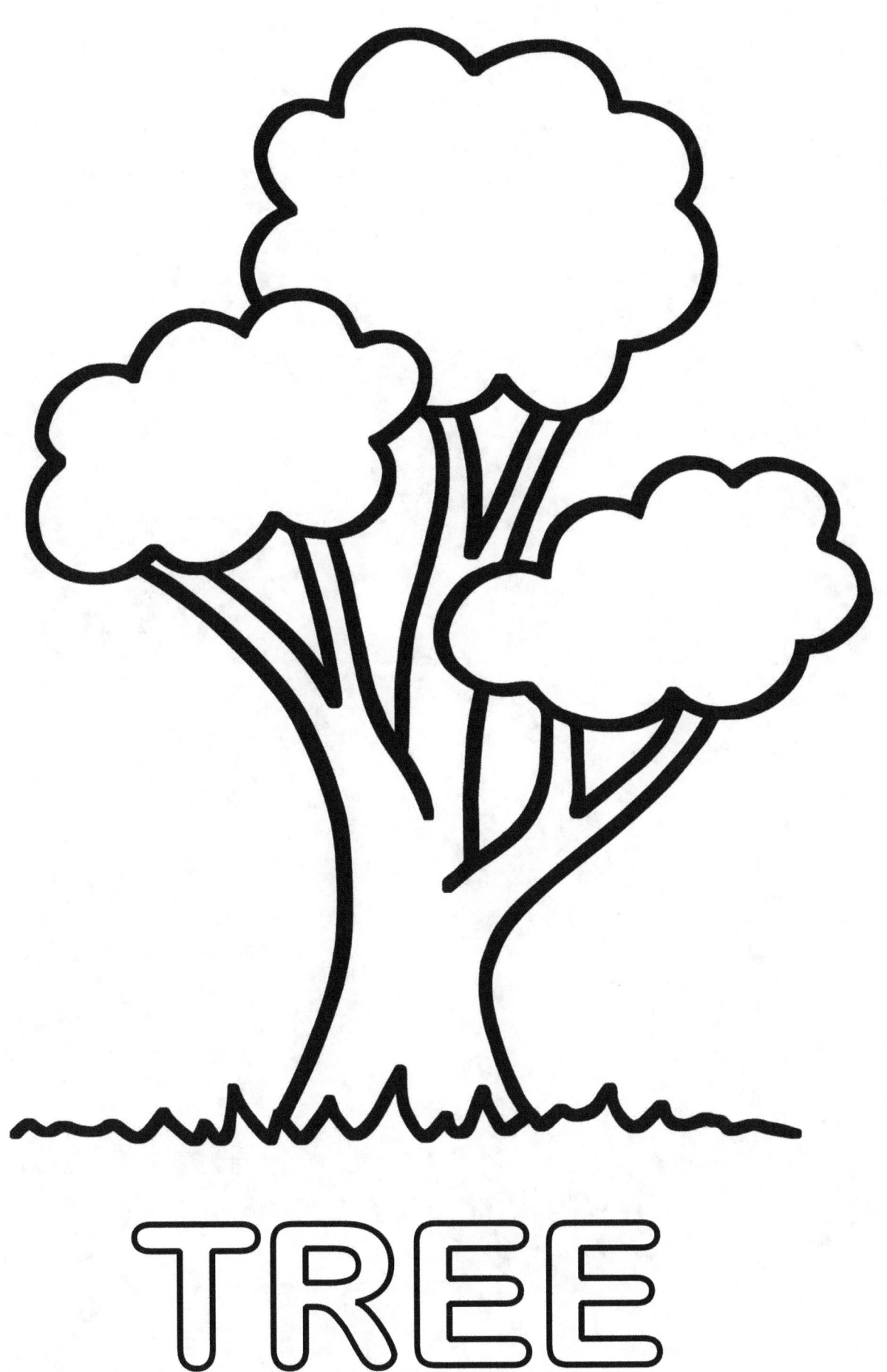

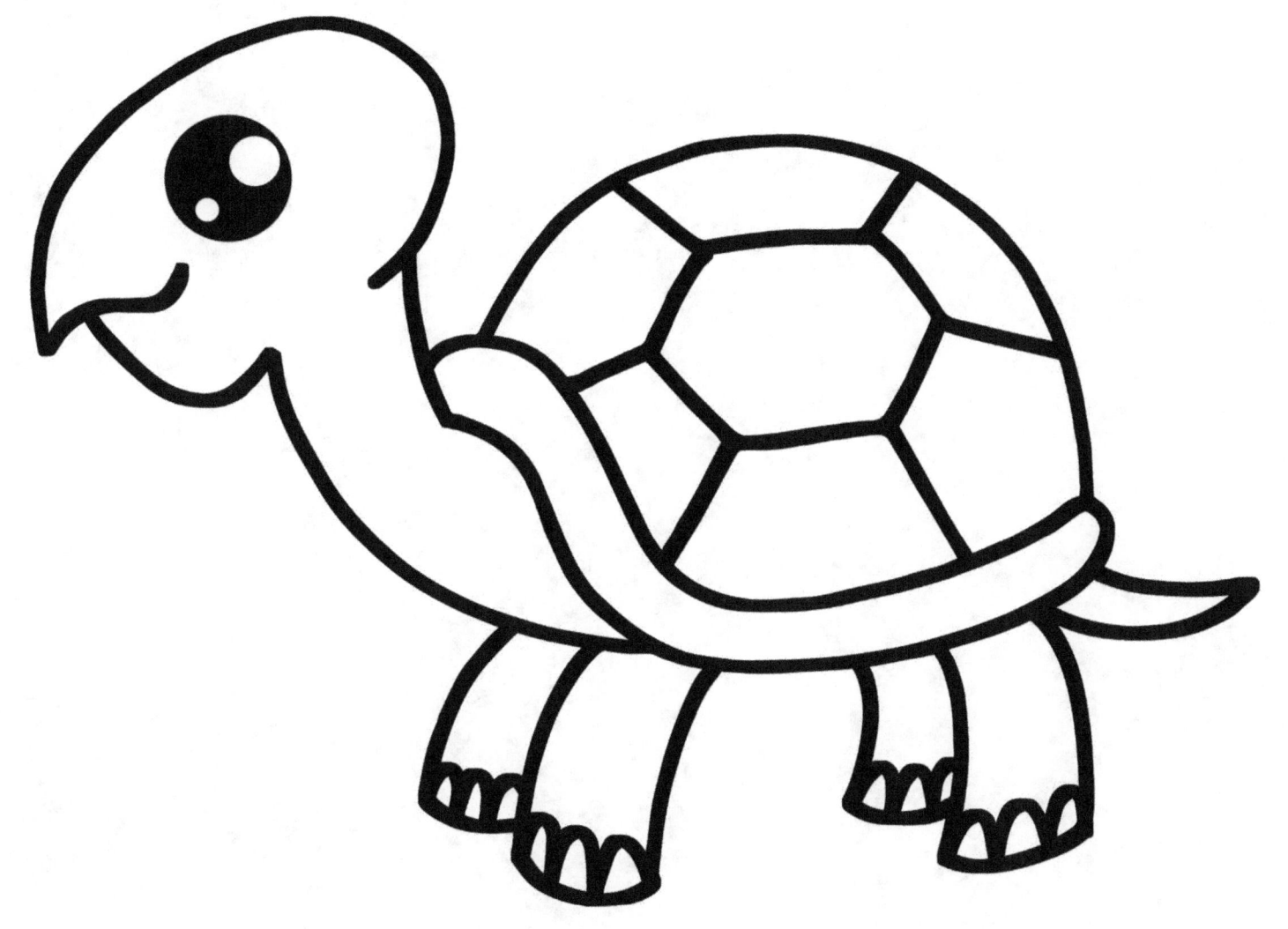

TURTLE

TURTLE

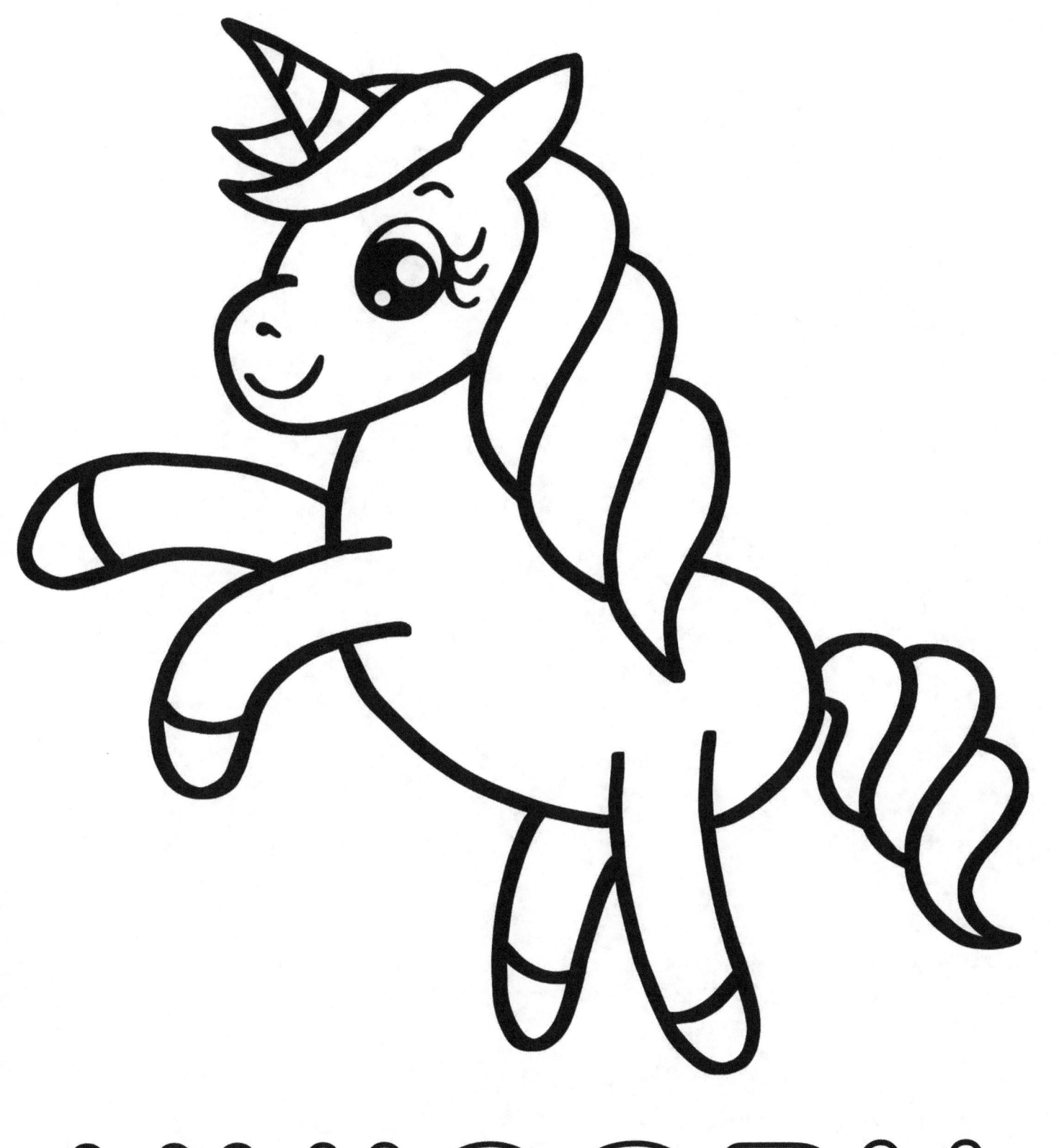

About

The Coloring Book for Toddlers is part of a series of books created by ToyToons. ToyToons is a youtube channel dedicated to how to draw videos for kids.

▶ **How to Draw Videos:** YouTube.com/ToyToons
▶ **Step by Step Drawings:** DrawingGuides.com

www.ingramcontent.com/pod-product-compliance
Lightning Source LLC
Chambersburg PA
CBHW080508220526
45465CB00006B/2414